GUARANTEED
GOALS

HOW TO GUARANTEE YOU SUCCEED
AT ANY GOAL YOU SET IN ADVANCE

JULLIEN GORDON
FOREWORD BY DOUG SUNDHEIM

**THIS BOOK WAS WRITTEN IN LESS THAN 30 DAYS
USING THE GUARANTEED GOAL SETTING PROCESS**

TABLE OF CONTENTS

FOREWORD

One of the clearest examples of the power of goals that I've ever seen is NASA's Apollo 13 mission. The mission operations team had to figure out how to get the astronauts home after the service module lost oxygen rendering it useless. The astronauts had to climb into the command module and start it up cold, something that had never been done or even practiced before. In three days, flight controllers developed and documented new procedures that would normally take three months. But it *had* to happen. Lives were on the line and as Gene Kranz famously said, "Failure is not an option."

As the co-author of the best selling *The 25 Best Time Management Tools & Techniques*, I can tell you that setting Guaranteed Goals is an extremely important component of success. Given my 15 years of experience as a leader, I've always been amazed at what human beings are capable of when they simply must make something happen. In this book, Jullien shows you how to create must win situations where failure is not an option. We've all been there before— down by a point or two with only a few seconds on the clock, or an hour left before a paper is due. Somehow, in these situations, we're able to summon a level of focus and effort that we didn't know we had. We surprise ourselves, and in the process, shift the horizon of what we see as possible.

Guaranteed Goals aims to help you transform what you thought was possible for your life by giving you a process and set of tools to *make things happen*. We all know that simply wanting things to be different never gets us very far. We've got to pave the road of good intentions with bricks of action if we want to reach our goals. However, that's often easier said than done. Our personal and professional success requires commitment and accountability. Thankfully, Jullien has created an easy to use goal setting process that will increase your motivation to achieve your goals.

One of the wonderful things Jullien has done with this book is start from the assumption that the forces that keep us from our goals are not going away. Procrastination and perfection aren't going anywhere soon. Instead of suggesting we get rid of these tendencies, he makes the case that we should *use* them. In the pages ahead, you'll learn to make the good excuses to achieve your goals that outweigh your bad excuses for not achieving them. Jullien teaches you how to tip the balance and escape individual inertia by setting your goal in motion and thus, setting yourself on the road to success one month at a time.

Like all good ideas, they only become great if you use them. I heartily recommend that you experiment with Jullien's revolutionary ideas laid out in his Guaranteed Goal Setting process in your life. It will take the bad excuses out of your life and make your months, years, and life extraordinary.

Doug Sundheim
Author of *The 25 Best Time Management Tools & Techniques: How To Get More Done Without Driving Yourself Crazy*

PREFACE

"Excuses are monuments of nothingness. They build bridges to nowhere. Those who use these tools of incompetence, seldom become anything but nothing at all."

—Unknown

Guaranteed Goals work for all types of goals including personal, professional, spiritual, educational, financial, and health. It could be something you need to start, stop, or go harder on. It may be something you need to invest in (an instrument software, a class, training, lessons, video cam) or something that you need to stop investing in like smoking, fast food consumption, or being late. It could be a relationship with an organization or person that you need to end (i.e. board seat, job, volunteer, etc) or one you need to begin (mentor, leadership role, ToastMasters, your own company, etc).

Consider yourself warned. I push. I push people to their greatness, to their highest self, to their full potential, to their purpose. I believe that if you love something you should push it and if it comes back to you, you should push it harder. Just the other day, I helped someone land their dream job after months of unemployment because I encouraged her to set a Guaranteed Goal to create a blog related to the industry she wanted to work in. In 30 days, she completed ten blog posts displaying her expertise and enhancing her personal brand. Here's what she wrote me after getting the job:

I can help you get to where you want to go faster. I believe that we should not put off until tomorrow what we can do today. Therefore, I continue to challenge *society's schedules* and timelines. It's time to get off society's "Simon Says" schedule and onto your own. If you do what everyone else does, you'll end up exactly where everyone else ends up.

Over the course of a lifetime, we can accomplish almost anything. But it hurts me when I see people living on the *deferred life plan* where they put off goals that can be easily accomplished in a focused period of time for later. If you ever wanted to know how the early bird gets the worm, then you're reading the right book. By using Guaranteed Goal Setting, I'm going to show you how you can end procrastination and perfectionism forever.

Guaranteed Goal Setting will transform the way you set goals and eliminate all of your excuses until none are left. This process will help you achieve a healthy rhythm for your life that allows you to accomplish 12 powerful things in a year rather than nothing at all. It will help you create a support system for yourself and your goals through community accountability. And it will help you accomplish whatever it is that you want faster than you would on your own.

This book was written in 30 days using the same goal setting process that I'm going to teach you. I developed the Guaranteed Goals book as a quick and easy-to-use system for you to get to where you want to go in life. Below are a few examples of how people are using the three principles of Guaranteed Goals—Authenticity, Accountability, and Activation—to transform their lives. After reading them, you will see how simple it is to start your own.

CHANGE JOBS OR CAREERS

AUTHENTICITY: Your first job out of college wasn't what you expected and you're ready for a change. Instead of being unemployed or underemployed, you want to find a career that you are passionate about.

ACCOUNTABILITY: To avoid jumping from the frying pan into the fire, you organize an evening for professionals you trust and respect including friends and mentors.

ACTIVATION: During the evening, you present your 30 second pitch, your resume, your self-analysis (strengths, skills, passions) and ask for referrals, feedback, and advice. To prepare for your event, you put yourself through a period of self-evaluation so that you can equip them with what they need to help you successfully land a job you like.

GO TO GRADUATE SCHOOL

AUTHENTICITY: After working for a few years after college, you decide that you want to go back to graduate school.

ACCOUNTABILITY: You set a 30 day Guaranteed Goal to invite your friends and mentors over for dinner to offer you feedback on your purpose statement and story.

ACTIVATION: At your dinner, you can present to them your purpose statement, school research, and receipt of registration for the appropriate entrance exam (i.e. GRE, GMAT, MCAT, LSAT). This would be the appropriate time to ask for feedback, support, ideas, and letters of recommendations.

GENERATE PASSIVE INCOME

AUTHENTICITY: A client of mine wanted to double his income in a month. At the time, he was making $3,000 a month and he wanted to double it to $6,000. Instead of trying to make that jump in one month, we created a Guaranteed Goal to increase his understanding of how to make money first.

ACCOUNTABILITY: At the end of the month, he was required to make a short presentation to others and myself about his effort to sell something everyday for 30 days straight. He could sell anything—a piece of gum, a used book online, consulting services, domain names, or art. The presentation would include how much he made and what he learned about himself and value creation.

ACTIVATION: To set the goal in motion, all he had to do was grab an old book off of his shelf and post it on Craigslist and

Ebay and put it at a very competitive price to get his first sell. He admits that he wouldn't have thought of this alone—that's what the power of the collective Guaranteed Goals Group's wisdom offers. I got the idea from this guy who started with one red paper clip and bartered his way up to a house (oneredpaperclip.blogspot.com). I just wanted my client to focus on selling for one month so that he could increase his understanding of value creation and marketing.

TACKLE A TERM PAPER

AUTHENTICITY: It's the first day of the semester and you already have a term paper due in 4 weeks. Your goal is to get it done on time without procrastinating.

ACCOUNTABILITY: On the second day of the semester, schedule two meetings with your professor or teacher's assistant; one to review the first draft and one to review the second draft.

ACTIVATION: By establishing the meetings, you now have another person holding you accountable to your goals and are less likely to procrastinate. By mid-semester, you'll have 80% of the paper done already, while most of your classmates are still considering their topic.

SHARE YOUR PASSION

AUTHENTICITY: Say for instance, you're a musician who wants to release an album by a certain date and you are committed to spreading the positive messages you write and sing.

ACCOUNTABILITY: Instead of just secretly writing the date on a calendar, Guaranteed Goal Setting suggests that you host a living room listening party or live performance a week or two before you want the actual CD to be done and send invitations to 30 friends and close fans anticipating that 5-10 of them will come.

ACTIVATION: By creating the event, you've set something in motion and created a good excuse to complete the songs. Now you have to get ready, and that forces (in a good way) you to create and finish the music you want to spread.

Below are some more Guaranteed Goals people have used to move forward. If your Guaranteed Goal is to be a better public speaker, then your 30 Day Do It may be to give a 5 minute speech on a topic that you are passionate about at your Guaranteed Goals Group. It could be a demonstration, presentation, question and answer session, performance, sharing photos, showing a video, or distributing a document you created. Essentially, you are creating a curriculum for yourself that encourages lifelong learning and your program is the space to demonstrate what you've learned about yourself and a particular subject or skill.

The purpose of goal setting is ultimately lifestyle design. We set a goal when we want to see a change in who we are being, how we are doing, and what we are having. Many people live their life by default, not by design— their life choices (or lack there of) were made based on proximity, convenience, comfort, and what other people were doing. But we eventually come to realize unintentional living is unfulfilling. That's when we set and commit to a new goal.

You can create your own Guaranteed Goal or you can visit WWW.GUARANTEEDGOALS.COM to find 30 Day Do It programs created by experts in a variety of fields such as: personal finance, education, entrepreneurship, professional development, personal branding, health, cooking and more.

MORE EXAMPLES OF GUARANTEED GOALS

Guaranteed Goal	30 Day Do It Program
Write a book	Create a reading at your home for your 1st draft with 4 friends.
Lose 10 lbs	Buy the dress you can't fit in but want to in 30 days and organize a dinner party at your house where you will wear the dress no matter what happens.
Quit your job	Have a friend organize a surprise "I Quit My Job" party for you after a certain date that you declare to quit by.
Run a marathon	Pay for your registration, join a training group, and organize a celebration among friends at the finish line or on the evening of the race.
Lead a workshop	Send an invitation to 5 friends right now for a trial version of the workshop in 30 days. This will force you to get the curriculum ready. (I used this process for my Driving School for Life course and since then, I've led the course 15 times in 5 cities for 200 people.)
Blog weekly	Invite friends to your blog launch party where you will reveal your blog and share why you created it. You can use www.lettermelater.com to send emails out today that will be automatically delivered 30 days from now. This is irreversible which forces you to get ready.
Start a business	Enter a business plan competition with a team of people. You'll end up with a business plan and a whole new awareness about your business from the experience even if you don't win.
Move cities	Go online today, buy your one-way plane ticket, and call the movers to move you one month from today.

INTRODUCTION

"A New Year's resolution is something that goes in one year and out the other."
— Unknown

When we create our goals for the year, they usually include goals we didn't accomplish last year in addition to new goals. After 365 days, how is it possible that we are in the exact same place as we were the year before?

In answering this question, we make a lot of bad excuses about why we didn't achieve our goals in the previous year. These excuses speak to the reasons why we failed. Sometimes our excuses sound *good* (i.e. My computer crashed the night before the presentation to the CEO) and sometimes they sound bad. **Regardless of how our excuses *sound*, they are excuses nonetheless.** Behind all of the excuses, the real reason most goals don't get accomplished is because we aren't compelled by the reason *why* we set them in the first place.

As we seek to achieve our goals, life puts unexpected obstacles in our way to test how bad we truly want it. If losing 50 pounds or making one million dollars was easy, then they probably wouldn't be our goals. **We set goals to challenge ourselves to grow in a variety of ways.** We usually want to stop something, start something, stick to something, or see something new in our lives. **Since satisfaction in all aspects of our lives is our ultimate goal, dissatisfaction is actually the catalyst for new goals.** We tend to make a decision to change once we are dissatisfied to the point that we can't take it anymore and our tolerance level has been peaked. My goal is to remove any excuse that may prevent you from finishing this book and learning this powerful goal setting process that will allow you to finish anything you start.

GUARANTEED GOALS

Guaranteed Goals is an "advanced" goal setting strategy that leverages the power of authenticity, accountability, and a activation to help you achieve your goals in less time. Advanced is literal and figurative. This strategy is all about how you setup the goal in advance of taking action and it's not for beginners who are comfortable just writing their goals down with dates. By simply changing the sequence of events that make up the goal setting and goal achievement process, you can significantly increase the likelihood that you will achieve any goal you set. The main differences between old goals and Guaranteed Goals are as follows:

PRINCIPLES: GUARANTEED GOALS VS. OLD GOALS

	Guaranteed Goals Principles	Old Goals Principles
Authenticity: Clarify Why This & Why Now	Why?	Wow!
	30 Days (i.e. Every 3rd Thursday)	365 Days (i.e. Birthday or New Year's)
	12 Small New Month's Resolutions	A Few Big New Year's Resolutions
Accountability: Create Positive Peer Pressure	Event-Based	Date-Based
	Celebrate On...	Celebrate If...
	Public & Peers	Private & Personal
Activation: Find The First Domino & Burn The Boats	The First Domino	Chronological Order
	Input Focused	Outcome Focused

Guaranteed Goals are a form of structured procrastination, a term coined by John Perry to explain various strategies that people can use to mitigate the degree to which they procrastinate. As much as we say we hate structure when we have it, sometimes we need it. After formal education ends, there is no structure to our personal life outside of work. Structure is a form of discipline and lack of self-discipline is the reason many people end up with the same New Year's resolutions year after year.

When you're in school for 12 to 16 years, you feel the need to rebel against structure. "I can't wait until I graduate" or "I can't wait until I'm free." In reality, most people crave structure. If you had 365 days to spend doing whatever you wanted, you probably wouldn't know what to do with yourself. You see this with recent retirees all of the time. We like schedules and plans because they remove uncertainty by allowing us to know what's next. If we could only apply the same structure we adhere to in school or work to our personal lives, our New Year's resolutions would actually be *new* every year.

When I was in business school, I had an idea for a new internet business. So I partnered with some of my classmates who specialized in areas of business that complemented my strengths and the needs for the business and we entered a business plan competition. The first round required capturing the essence of the business to the best of our ability in a 2-page executive summary. Once we advanced to the second round, we were required to write an entire business plan within a month. Finally, we had to make a pitch to an esteemed group of judges to compete for the $10,000 cash prize.

The structure of the business plan competition forced my team to put our thoughts on paper. By establishing unmovable deadlines and requiring us to present in front of a panel, we completed all the research, strategy, financial and market analysis necessary for a complete business plan. We ended up placing third and winning $3,000, but the business plan that we wrote allowed us to raise more capital within the next 6 months. Though every team goes in with the purpose of winning the money, only one team gets the grand prize. On the other hand, every team leaves with a business plan that is at least 80% right that they can use to attract financing for their idea. The business plan competition served as a Guaranteed Goal to complete our business plan.

By creating a little structure, the business plan competition got my team to accomplish more in a shorter amount of time than it would have taken us if we tried to do it on our own. Having outside judges also increased the quality of our work. The competition set our goal in motion and the simple checkpoints kept the momentum alive. The moment we signed up for the competition, a series of events were activated that moved us from a few guys with a good idea to an official company.

Guaranteed Goals also mitigate perfectionism by accepting that all first versions presented at your Guaranteed Goals Group are only 80% right. One of the purposes of the Guaranteed Goals Group is to increase your quality of work and give you feedback to move from 80% to 100% complete. When "complete" isn't defined, goals tend to linger because of perfectionism—a fear that something is less complete than it actually is. Most projects are slow to start because of procrastination (or individual inertia) or slow to finish because of perfectionism. Some people start strong and end weak while others start weak and end strong. Both paths are forms of procrastination and perfectionism.

Perfectionism and procrastination are merely two-sides of the same coin. **Perfectionism is the over commitment of time and energy to the successful completion of a goal and procrastination is the under commitment of time and energy.** Perfectionism isn't inherently bad. It is only detrimental when it causes us to spend more time on a project than is warranted out of fear of failure. **Perfection is relative and the goal is for your performance to be seen as high quality in your own eyes and the eyes of the observer.** This is why feedback is so important to the Guaranteed Goal Setting process and that getting something 80% right is the main emphasis of the process rather than perfection.

Procrastination is characterized by the deferment of actions or tasks to a later time. There is nothing wrong with deferring a goal as long as you can accurately estimate and allocate the appropriate amount of time it will take you to complete the goal. But anyone who has tried to guess which lane will move fastest at the grocery store or on the highway knows that in many cases we are wrong about our estimations of time. Procrastination becomes detrimental when you underestimate how long it will actually take to produce a high-quality end product. Guaranteed Goal Setting is designed to mitigate perfectionism and procrastination so that you can successfully complete your goals on time.

OLD GOAL SETTING

To be honest, there isn't much wrong with traditional goal setting. In fact, it works for those who are self-disciplined and have a clear sense of purpose, which garners self-discipline. When you are clear on the reason *why* you're doing something and that reason moves you internally, self-discipline naturally kicks in to help. **Self-discipline is only perceived as negative when you are being disciplined to do something that you don't see as purposeful.** The main problem I see with traditional goal setting is that the sequence of the steps can be reordered to produce better results.

Old Goal Setting Process

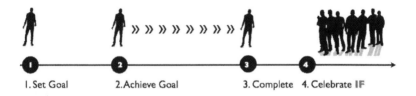

1. Set Goal   2. Achieve Goal   3. Complete   4. Celebrate **IF**

Guaranteed Goal Setting Process

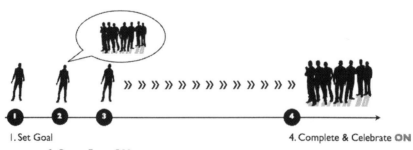

1. Set Goal   4. Complete & Celebrate **ON**

2. Create Event **ON**

SEQUENCE: GUARANTEED GOALS VS. OLD GOALS

Guaranteed Goals Process	Old Goals Process
1. Set Goal: Choose what you want to accomplish.	**1. Set Goal:** Choose what you want to accomplish, perhaps in writing.
2. Create Event ON: Send out an invitation to your celebration up front to activate your goal. Plan like you're going to achieve it.	**2. Achieve Goal:** Break the goal down into actionable items or a to do list and start checking things off.
3. Achieve Goal: Break the goal down into actionable items or a to-do list and start with the first domino.	**3. Complete Goal**: Check off the final box on your to-do list.
4. Complete Goal & Celebrate ON: Do whatever it takes to complete your goal and demonstrate that you achieved the goal by presenting some sort of evidence at your celebration.	**4. Celebrate IF:** If you achieve the goal, perhaps plan a celebration.

The comparison above shows you the difference between old goals and Guaranteed Goals. In its simplest form, the process for Guaranteed Goal Setting is as follows:

GUARANTEED GOALS PROCESS

1. AUTHENTICITY: Clarify Why This & Why Now
2. ACCOUNTABILITY: Create Positive Peer Pressure
3. ACTIVATION: Find The First Domino & Burn The Boats

The next few chapters will explain each step in detail and address the how and *why* of each step, but before that I want to guide you through the creation of your first Guaranteed Goal.

YOUR FIRST GUARANTEED GOAL

Rather than having you read the book first to assess whether or not the Guaranteed Goals will radically transform your life, I thought it would be best to prove it to you by having you set a Guaranteed Goal right now to finish reading the book. If you haven't finished any book you've started reading in a while, this will be a great challenge and opportunity to change.

1. AUTHENTICITY: Clarify Why This & Why Now

First and foremost, I need you to take a moment to write down one sentence clarifying why you want to finish reading this book:

Example: I want to accomplish all of my 20___ goals and look back on this year with no regrets.

....

....

....

....

2. ACCOUNTABILITY: Create Positive Peer Pressure

The next step is to set your goal in motion. I want you to create a Guaranteed Goals Group at your house within the next 30 days. I can hear the excuses now. "My house isn't clean.I don't have enough space. I can't think of anyone to invite. I'm busy." Yadi dadi da. Are you done yet? (Smiley face).

I'm glad that you shared all of those excuses with me because I see them as great reasons for you to host a Guaranteed Goals Group. Not only will you finish reading this book, you will also have the opportunity to clean your house, throw stuff away to create more space in your life, deepen relationships with a few of your friends, and free your schedule to do something that matters to you.

It's time to stop prioritizing your schedule and start scheduling your priorities. Before reading any further, take 10 minutes to complete the following action items:

1. Set a date and time. The event should occur on or before your 30 day mark.

2. Edit and send the invitation below to about 1-10 people depending on how comfortable you feel. If you want to start off small, just invite a couple friends. If you want to challenge yourself even more, invite 10 people with the expectation that only half of the people will accept the invitation. You can either send it as is using your regular email account, or try a service such as Evite.com, Pingg.com, or Facebook Events. And don't forget to invite me at jullien@newhigher.com.

3. ACTIVATION: Find The First Domino & Burn The Boats
Now that the invitation is sent, you have 30 days or less to execute by finishing reading this book and preparing for your Guaranteed Goals Group. You should set aside time to read 20 pages per day for the next week, clean, and go to the grocery store to buy some snacks and drinks for your group members.

SAMPLE EMAIL INVITATION

SUBJECT:
Goal Setting Party At My House, Wed. 7-8:30pm

BODY:

Hello Friends,

It doesn't have to be New Year's Eve to think about your goals—they should be on your mind at all times. If you've been procrastinating but have some personal or professional goals that you want to get done, then join me at my house on Wednesday night at 7pm.

Bring your New Year's resolutions or any other goals written down. I will provide the goal setting materials and some food, but feel free to bring something if you would like.

Please RSVP so that I can get a head count.

Cheers!

Your Name
Your Address
Your Phone Number

When the day comes, it's up to you to facilitate and share the Guaranteed Goal Setting process. The program for the evening should go as follows:

SAMPLE INITIAL MEETING AGENDA

Time	Agenda Item	Action Item
7:00-7:15	**Welcome**	What's your name? What are your goals? What's stopping you?
7:15-7:30	**Introduction**	What's Guaranteed Goal Setting? How does it work? Why? Where?
7:30-7:45	**Worksheets**	Put old goals into the Guaranteed Goals framework
7:45-8:00	**Presentations**	Everyone present and get approval on their Guaranteed Goal
8:00-8:15	**Celebration**	Agree on the time and place for the next Guaranteed Goals Group meeting & celebration
8:15-8:30	**Feedback**	What worked? What didn't?

After this initial meeting, on a given day every month (i.e. every third Thursday), you and your peers, team, or colleagues should set aside 60 to 90 minutes to celebrate and hold each other accountable for each other's goals. The purpose of the space is to:

1. Allow each goal setter to do a short 5 minute presentation on his or her 30 Day Do It from the month before.

2. Set a new Guaranteed Goal and 30 Day Do It for the next month.

3. Agree on a date, time, and location for the next 30 Day Do It group meeting.

25

The agenda for the monthly 30 Day Do It meeting thereafter could look as follows:

SAMPLE MONTHLY AGENDA

Time	Agenda Item	Action Item
5 min	Greeting by John	Welcome by the host
10 min	Individual Evaluations	Complete the Guaranteed Goal Evaluation Worksheet
5 min	Presentation #1 by Max	Max steps on the scale to show he lost 5 pounds
5 min	Presentation #2 by Emily	Emily reveals her 3 new paintings
5 min	Presentation #3 by Shane	Shane shows us before and after pictures of his blog and how he developed his personal brand
5 min	Presentation #4 by Brandy	Brandy reads the 1st chapter of her upcoming book
5 min	Presentation #5 by Phil	Phil shares what he learned about his purpose through daily meditation and reading
5 min	Presentation #6 by John	John shares his career transition plan and shows printouts of emails he sent
10 min	New Goals	Complete the Guaranteed Goal Setting Worksheet
10 min	Approval	Everyone shares their new Guaranteed Goal and gets approval or challenged by the group
5 min	Feedback	Host requests feedback on the evening
5 min	Next 30 Day Do It	Set a date and location for the next one
75 min		

For example, say Person #1's Guaranteed Goal is to lose 60 pounds this year, then their 30 Day Do It for each month would be to lose 5 pounds. On January 1st, they should weigh themselves to identify their starting point. Their presentation should require bringing the same scale to each Guaranteed Goals Group to demonstrate that they achieved their goal for the month. They should share with the group what went right, what went wrong, and how they think they can improve next month based on their self-discoveries documented on the Guaranteed Goal Evaluation Worksheet.

By simply committing to this 60 to 90 minutes of accountability and renewal each month, I'm certain that any goal you truly desire to achieve that is a function of your effort—as opposed to luck or the actions of others—can be accomplished. **Effort is a function of our time, and time is our most valuable resource. How we choose to spend our time is the only true decision we have in each moment.** Therefore, if your Guaranteed Goal is to increase your income by $1,000,000 in a month, though I believe it is possible, you must demonstrate how the reallocation of your time can potentially lead to that outcome. Over the course of a year, your Guaranteed Goals Group meetings will require less than 24 hours (90 minutes x 12 months = 18 hours) of time to make sure you spend the other 364 days of your year accomplishing your goals.

Guaranteed Goals Groups are one form of structure that you can use for your personal and professional goals. It doesn't matter how you choose to celebrate or demonstrate your goal achievement as long as it is consistent and easy to organize. Similar to school, these spaces help close the loop between preparation, performance, and improvement so that you can understand your successful and unsuccessful patterns. The benefit of Guaranteed Goals Groups is that the collective wisdom and accountability of the group helps you create interesting 30 Day Do It programs that are fun and exciting for everyone to do and witness.

ESCALATION OF COMMITMENT

Commitment is the reason we see goals through the end, but it is hard to commit when you don't know your *why*. Commitment is key but it is also rare and almost non-existent in our relationships to ourselves, our ideas, our purpose, our families, our place of living, and our employers. According to Jennifer Baker of the Forest Institute of Professional Psychology in Springfield, Missouri, 50% of first marriages, 67% of second and 74% of third marriages end in divorce. Basically, when one commitment is broken, the likelihood of the next commitment ending increases. The U.S. Department of Labor estimates that today's learner will have 10-14 jobs by the age of 38, whereas our parents sought out lifetime employment from one employer. As a result, people are moving around more, never committing to one community for more than three years. I've personally had five addresses in four cities since finishing college six years ago. However, there are some simple ways to increase commitment to your goals, employing a couple of strategies integrated into the Guaranteed Goal Setting process.

A1955 study by Deutsch and Gerard examined students' commitments to their initial word. Students were required to estimate the length of lines they were shown. They divided the students into three sample groups:

» **PUBLIC:** Commit publicly by writing down their estimate, signing their name, and giving the paper to the experimenter.

» **PRIVATE:** Commit privately by writing down their estimate on a Magic Pad and then erasing their answer before anyone could see it.

» **NO COMMITMENT:** Just keep initial estimate privately in their mind.

Next, all students were given new evidence that led them to believe that their initial estimates were wrong and they had the opportunity to change their estimates. Those in the group most resistant to change were the ones who made their commitments in writing and publicly. Even when new evidence was revealed after their commitment, participants behaved in an irrational way. The students in the first group demonstrate a term called *escalation of commitment,* introduced by Barry M. Staw in his 1976 paper, "Knee deep in the big muddy: A study of escalating commitment to a chosen course of action." It is defined as the phenomenon where people justify increased investment in a decision, based on the cumulative prior investment, despite new evidence, which may suggest that the initial decision was wrong. An example would be gambling away half of your life savings and then trying to win it back by gambling with the other half. Despite your awareness that the probabilities of winning are always in favor of the casino, you continue to bet your life savings to avoid losing and you end up losing even more. The term is often used to describe poor decision-making in projects especially in business and government.

In most cases, escalation of commitment is seen as a bad thing, but I believe it can be used for good. Escalation of commitment leads to poor decisions when there is "new evidence suggesting that the decision was probably wrong," but goals aren't about right and wrong—they are about what you want. **Guaranteed Goals require that you identify your *why* up front so that you can ensure that the goal is right for you.** Most goals aren't inherently wrong, though a person's means to accomplish them may be flawed. Typically, the consequences of not accomplishing your goals is minimal—you simply end up where you were when you set them. Though we may say we want change every year, our actions speak louder than our words. Many people start the New Year exactly where they left off the year before because their desire to change lacked purpose. So if you really want change in your life, Guaranteed Goals is the way to create it because it builds in your commitment up front by turning your words into immediate action.

Commitment has to do with an investment of time and energy into whatever it is you are committed to. In order to get anything or anywhere, it will likely require these elements. Any goal we choose is the result of a cost-benefit analysis. We ask ourselves "Am I willing to pay A to get (to) Z? Am I willing to endure this pain to get this pleasure?" In his book, *Need to Know*, business-building expert Paul Myers puts it best when he says:

"Make the pleasures that you get and the pain you avoid when you achieve your goal as strong as you can. Then make the pleasure you get and the pain you avoid by NOT getting it as weak as possible."

If the benefit or pleasure is greater than the cost or pain, then you go for it. If it's equal, you're indifferent. And if the perceived cost is greater than the perceived benefit then you don't do it, even if it is good for you.

TIPPING THE BALANCE

Many people are experts at starting goals, but novices at finishing them. Some people resort to incentives to tip the balance between the perceived costs and benefits of starting and finishing a goal. **Incentives are one way to motivate yourself and others, but they are only effective if the person wants more *and* values the incentive.** Whereas a financial bonus may motivate some people, others may value time and simply want an additional day off. Through my experience as a leader, I've discovered that incentives without disincentives are futile if people are content where they already are. **By having incentives and disincentives, you force yourself or others to make a choice— otherwise people tend to stand still. One must create a scenario where if you do nothing you lose and if you do something you win. In this scenario, standing still is not an option.**

Unfortunately, for most goals, the cost is greater than or equal to the benefit and that's why you haven't done them yet. In order to increase the perceived costs or benefits, you need to clarify your ***why***. When the why is clear, it serves as a magnet that pulls you toward the goal or vision. Clarifying the ***why*** taps into your infinite well of intrinsic motivation, which comes from rewards inherent to the task or activity itself. **Clarifying your *why* is free, but incentives cost.**

In the book, *A Psychology of Ultimate Concern*, Hetty Zock states "A balanced ratio between a sense of initiative and a sense of guilt results in the strength of purpose: the possibility of being after something, of striving towards a goal, without being unduly inhibited." My high school basketball coach exhibited this philosophy perfectly to improve our free throw shooting. Every practice, there was a free throw shooting drill where each player on the 13 man team would have to make two free throws. The rest of the team lined up on the baseline under the hoop. If the person missed a free throw, everyone would have to sprint the distance of the court and back. This would continue until everyone made two free throws. By the time we were all done, we could have sprinted the court's length up to 30 times. The coach tipped the balance. He increased the cost of missing a free throw from one person's personal embarrassment to personal embarrassment in the eyes of 12 teammates plus physical conditioning plus collective frustration! I'm sure that even if we made 26 straight free throws he would have found a way to make us run, but this way he wasn't the target of our grunts and cold stares.

Think of your goals like a weighing scale—on one side are the costs of pursuing your goal and on the other side are the benefits of achieving your goal. You have the power to tip the balance. Rather than ending up right where you are a year from now if you don't accomplish your goals, you can create a scenario for yourself that changes the costs and benefits of achieving your goal. This is important because for most goals, the cost equals the benefit, which means that we're indifferent. For example, the 100 hours of relaxation time that you may have to give up to research and write a book is equally valuable to you as being a published author, so you choose to stay on the couch. When the costs are greater than the benefits, you don't move at all and when the benefits are greater than the costs, you move. This applies to all areas of life including shopping, dating, investing, traveling, and more.

WEIGHING THE COSTS & BENEFITS

COSTS *greater than* BENEFITS

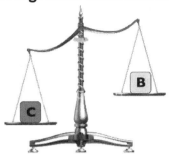

NO MOVE. DON'T EVEN START GOAL.

COSTS *less than* BENEFITS

MOVE. ACCOMPLISH GOAL.

COSTS *equals* BENEFITS

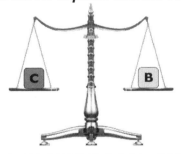

INDIFFERENT. MAY START GOAL, BUT UNLIKELY TO
FINISH. MOST NEW GOALS ARE HERE.

To tip the balance, you have your intrinsic and extrinsic desires that you can place on each side of the scale so that the benefits outweigh the costs. For instance, you could increase the costs of not achieving your goal by giving a friend a $200 check to keep and cash if you fail or to tear up and trash if you prevail. You could increase the benefits by vowing to go shopping for a new wardrobe if you achieve your weight loss goals for clothes that fit. **It's time to stop betting that things will change and start betting on yourself that you will be the change you want to see.**

Below is an example of how I tipped the balance to write this book in 30 days. The main reasons we create goals are for feelings, actions, money, or time, so here is how I assessed my goal of writing this book:

1. I began by writing in the benefits of doing the goal and the costs of doing the goal in columns two and three from a feeling, action, money, and time perspective. You may not have something for every box. Sometimes, we can't articulate a benefit or cost and therefore we can't account for it either.

2. Then, I ranked everything 1 to 3 according to their value to me. I don't value exhaustion or frustration, but I ranked them according to how much I would pay not to have them in my life.

3. Next, I added the benefits column and the cost columns separately and then compared the two numbers. If the benefits outweigh the costs, then I go for it. As you can see on the grey line, the benefits totaled +8 and the costs totaled -9.

GUARANTEED GOAL—WRITE A BOOK

	Benefits of Doing It	Value To You	Costs of Doing It	Value To You
FEELINGS spiritual/ emotional/ personal	*fulfilled & excited by helping people achieve their dreams, open to new ideas once this one is out*	+3	*exhausting, frustrating*	−2
ACTIONS passions/ people/social	*travel the world speaking, chance to write, start a movement*	+3	*less partying*	−2
MONEY	*maybe sell 1M copies*	+2	*$1,000s to print book*	−2
TIME	*(can't articulate)*	+	*100 hours of time*	−3
	TOTAL BENEFITS	+8	**TOTAL COSTS**	−9
additional commitment:	*promise my friends to cut my hair off if I don't send out a 1st draft by July 15th.*			
TIP THE BALANCE if necessary	*keep my hair*	+2		
		+10	**GREATER**	−9

4. If they don't, then I have to tip the balance by coming up with an additional benefit or creating a cost of *not* doing it. This forces me to make a choice and prevents me from having the option of ending up where I was before I set the goal. You can give the additional commitment to tip the balance a score of +/- 3 as well. In this case, I increased the benefit by +2 by making an additional commitment to my friends to cut my hair off if I didn't deliver. In this case, I made an additional commitment to cut off my which was a benefit of +2. The balance is tipped and now I take action.

Popular shows on television such as The Biggest Loser, America's Next Top Model, American Idol, and Dancing With The Stars have set up structures to help people do amazing things like lose weight, learn dances, improve their singing, or look better. Competitors have scheduled performances (or TV tapings) that they need to deliver on a certain date and are held accountable by the audience. The shows tap into contestants' intrinsic desires: status, fame, and acceptance; and their extrinsic desires: money, prizes, and most importantly their goal achievement.

Self-help guru Anthony Robbins said, "My definition of success is to live your life in a way that causes you to feel a ton of pleasure and very little pain - and because of your lifestyle, have the people around you feel a lot more pleasure than they do pain." Guaranteed Goals helps you structure your goals so that complete them is to your advantage and not completing them is to your disadvantage. By creating a game where you cannot end up in the same place as a result of inaction, you are more likely to move toward what you want and where you want to go.

CREATING YOUR OWN COSTS

What moves you doesn't move me. There is an assumption in goal setting, society, success, and leadership that the carrot that motivates you will equally motivate me. If that was the case, every student would work equally hard for a 4.0 GPA, every employee would work equally hard for a promotion or pay raise, or every citizen would abide by the laws. But that's not the case. One size does not fit all. Two people may value $1,000 potential prize differently. One person may be wiling to do anything they have to to get the $1,000 while another person may not share the same enthusiasm because they have different priorities, values, ambitions, or fears.

Given that, if the standard cost system doesn't motivate you, you have the power to create your own. There are 5 ways that you can tip the balance in a way that moves you if you don't complete your goal:

1. **Money:** Give up money to a cause you don't really like
2. **Time:** Give up time to a cause you don't really like
3. **Abstain:** Give up something you really like
4. **Physical:** Commit to do something physical
5. **Embarrassment:** Commit to do something embarrassing but bearable

Here is how to create your own cost system. Make an agreement with a friend that "If you don't write the first draft of your book in 30 days, you will take them to dinner at their favorite restaurant and not eat. Or you will donate $200 to a political party that you oppose. Or you will run a mile for every chapter you don't complete. Or you will wash 5 of your friends' cars by hand. Or you will give up social media and TV for one week. By simply making a agreement with an accountability partner, you've customized a cost system.

37

THE PHYSICS OF GOALS

Goal setting and goal achievement are two different legs of the same journey. Goal setting requires very little energy. The process of goal achievement is where the rubber meets the road. Goal setting is about thinking and writing whereas goal achievement is about movement and action. Therefore, to properly understand goal achievement, we must rewind back to our secondary school physics class to grasp some basic laws and vocabulary related to physical movement or motion.

Let's begin by refreshing your memory on Newton's three laws of motion. They are:

1. Every object in a state of uniform motion tends to remain in that state of motion unless an external force is applied to it.

2. Force applied on a body is directly proportional to the rate of change of momentum of the body or mass times acceleration (when proper units are chosen, $F = ma$).

3. Every action has an equal and opposite reaction.

The first law speaks to the concept of inertia, or the resistance of any physical object to a change its state of motion. In the same way, we are naturally resistant to change despite the fact that change is constant. We get comfortable with the pace of our lives and are resistant to increases and decreases.

No matter who you are, the resistance to change will arise. Guaranteed Goals helps you identify the action that will require the least amount of energy but make the biggest difference in your likelihood of achieving you goal. Sending a simple email or text invitation for your celebration sets an event in motion, other people in motion, and ultimately you in motion. The first step is the biggest!

The second law states that FORCE is equivalent to the MASS (or WEIGHT) times the acceleration (CHANGE in velocity over time). If you increase the mass and or acceleration of the object, the force increases making the movement more powerful.

When applied to Guaranteed Goals, the equation reads as follows. The extent to which you will be FORCED to complete your 30 Day Do It is equivalent to the MASS OF PEOPLE (or how many people are WAITING on you) times the CHANGE IN YOU over the time. Therefore, the more people you invite to your celebration and the greater the expected change in you, the more force you will put into achieving the goal.

Finally, the third law states that for every action, there is an equal and opposite reaction. Therefore, if you authentically go after your goals, things have to shift. Sometimes the shifts are visible (i.e. losing 10 lbs or getting a raise) but in most cases they are invisible because they are shifts in your attitudes, beliefs, and others' perceptions of you. For every authentic step you take towards your goals, the world reacts. On the other hand, your inaction will only result in other people's goals and visions being imposed on you.

With old goals, the reaction for success is celebration. If you don't celebrate yourself or others don't celebrate you when you succeed, there is still a reaction—you may work hard, you make work less hard, or you may get jaded for not being recognized. Still, the celebration only comes as a reaction to the performance.

39

Guaranteed Goals gets you to react to the celebration rather than the celebration being a reaction to your performance. By knowing that in 30 days, family, friends, colleagues, or members of your Guaranteed Goals Group will be at some event to celebrate your success changes your motivation and attitude about the goal at hand. The excellence of your execution will be directly correlated to the excellence of the event you set in motion, which will depend on how many people you invite, who you invite, and additional commitments you use to raise the stakes. **It's one thing to set goals. It's another thing to set them in motion.**

Physics defines force as any external agent that causes a change in the motion of a free body, or that causes stress in a fixed body. The force we are talking about here is an internal agent of change to force yourself to move on the things you've always wanted. If you are a fixed body, meaning that you haven't accomplished any of your goals recently, this process may cause a little stress as you are pushed beyond your perceived limits of yourself. But if your goals have a clear *why*, then it is better to be stressed in motion towards things you want rather than to be stressed about things that don't matter to you.

AUTHENTICITY:
Why This &
Why Now

Chapter 1

Why? vs. Wow!

"A man who becomes conscious of the responsibility he bears toward a human being who affectionately waits for him, or to an unfinished work, will never be able to throw away his life. He knows the 'why' for his existence, and will be able to bear almost any 'how.'"

— Victor Frankl

A lot of people have difficulty finishing things. You get off to a great start for one or two weeks—gym memberships skyrocket in January—and then you lose steam. The number one reason people don't finish what they start is because they lose sight of their *why*. Victor Frankl was an Austrian neurologist and psychiatrist, as well as a Holocaust survivor. His experience led him to write *Man's Search For Meaning* in which he says "A man who knows his *why* can bear almost any *how*." His observations recount that one of the keys to enduring the terrible conditions in the internment camps for himself and others was knowing their *why*. For Frankl, the hope of seeing his family was his *why*.

The x-factor of success is knowing your *why*. If your *why* is more compelling than your excuses, then your likelihood of accomplishing your goals is higher. Often, we simply write goals because they sound good and make others say "Wow." I call these ego-als. **Ego-als are lofty goals that sound fly like *eagles* but are primarily ego-driven.** They sound great, but have very little significance beyond the individual's pursuit. Oftentimes, ego-als aren't even personal; they are simply aggressive goals that one sets for themselves relative to their peer group. Research in positive psychology reveals that our happiness tends to be relative to our position in comparison to our peer group. As a result, ego-als have little to do with one's unique path and the pursuit of their purpose. Examples of ego-als include "I want to be a millionaire and retire by 35." or "I want to buy a house by the end of the year." It is deflating to pursue selfish goals that don't contribute to anyone else's life.

We create ego-als to fill the ego, but they are spiritually empty. When goals have a spiritual significance, our reason is clearer and our motivation is pure and therefore they are more likely to endure and be accomplished. I remember setting aggressive timelines for myself like the ones above until I realized that my timelines weren't based on anything except an age that I randomly selected. **Goals are important, but vision is even more important.** We need the crystal clear vision of eagles that can fly as high as 10,000 feet in the sky and then aggressively pursue their prey at 150 miles per hour. Vision gives our personal goals meaning. Goals without purpose and inner significance are harder to pursue and achieve than goals that have them.

INTRINSIC MOTIVATION

Professor Steven Reiss of Ohio State University is one of the world's leading thinkers on intrinsic motivation. His work is refreshing in a world driven by many external motivations, which may be legitimate, but not intrinsic. Based on studies of more than 6,000 people, he proposed a theory based on 16 basic desires that guide nearly all human behavior (See chart below). His theory allowed for two people to do the same thing for different reasons—one person may go to the gym primarily to exercise while another person may go primarily to socialize. Even if you have a similar goal to someone else, it's important to know your why, which allows you not to compare or compete just because the goal happens to be the same.

THE 16 BASIC DESIRES

» Acceptance: the need for approval	» Physical Activity: the need for exercise
» Curiosity: the need to think	» Power: the need for influence of will
» Eating: the need for food	» Romance: the need for sex
» Family: the need to raise children	» Saving: the need to collect
» Honor: the need to be loyal to the traditional values of one's clan/ ethnic group	» Social Contact, the need for friends (peer relationships)
» Idealism: the need for social justice	» Status: the need for social standing/ importance
» Independence, the need for individuality	» Tranquility: the need to be safe
» Order: the need for organized, stable, predictable environments	» Vengeance: the need to strike back

Now that you know your motives, the next step is your motion—that's where goal setting comes in. According to a GoalsGuy.com worldwide survey of 300,000 people, the top ten New Year's resolutions are as follows:

1. Lose Weight and Get in Better Physical Shape
2. Stick to a Budget
3. Debt Reduction
4. Enjoy More Quality Time with Family & Friends
5. Find My Soul Mate

6. Quit Smoking
7. Find a Better Job
8. Learn Something New
9. Volunteer and Help Others
10. Get Organized

This sounds like a great list and you've probably had a list that looked similar to it before, but this list is not spiritually sound until you are clear on your own **why** for a particular goal on the list. One method you may consider is connecting each of the ten resolutions above to one or two of the 16 desires that they satisfy. If you and I shared these goals, we may have different desires for doing them, but even still, selecting from a list of 16 desires doesn't personalize the goal to either of us. **I propose that you be clear about your larger purpose first and then clarify the purpose of each goal in relationship to your larger purpose. Only then will you be able to increase your fulfillment from year to year.** For example, if my purpose is to help other people find and align their lives with their purpose, none of the top 10 goals above specifically help me do that. If you want to lose weight, be able to explain what will be possible in your life by losing 20 pounds that isn't possible today.

William Damon of Stanford University has spent years researching purpose in youth. In his recent book *The Path To Purpose*, he defines the relationship between purpose and goals when he says, "A purpose is the reason behind the immediate goals and motives that drive most of our daily behavior." Purpose is a layer deeper than intrinsic desires. Damon says that "where no larger purpose exists, short-term goals and motives usually lead nowhere and soon extinguish themselves in directionless activity." Our goals should align us more and more with our purpose. You can quit smoking, find a better job, and lose 50 pounds and still feel directionless. This is what happens when we focus on *wow* instead of *why*.

It makes no sense to set goals before defining your life's purpose. The last thing I want is for you to accomplish thousands of things over the course of your lifetime, but fail to accomplish the one thing you were created to do. By beginning with your *why* and then setting purposeful goals, you can create meaningful movement that will align your life with your overall purpose. If you consider your purpose before setting new goals, you will realized that most New Year's resolutions and other goals you've probably been setting don't matter as much.

THE 8 CYLINDERS OF SUCCESSFUL GOAL SETTING

In my first book, *The 8 Cylinders of Success: How to Align your Personal & Professional Purpose*, I laid out a framework for how you can discover your life's purpose. The same principles that apply to the purpose of your life also applies to the purpose of your goals, projects, teams, and organizations. *The 8 Cylinders of Success*, is a decision-making tool for all areas of your life to ensure that your actions are aligned with your ultimate goal or purpose. Below is an example of how you can use *The 8 Cylinders of Success* to think through your goals to make sure that they are personally meaningful to you.

The missing *why* is the primary reason that bucket lists don't lead people to fulfillment. A bucket list is a list of things to do before someone "kicks the bucket" or dies. A bucket list may consist of activities like bungee jumping, sky diving, climbing to the top of Mount Everest, seeing the pyramids, driving a Shelby Mustang, or being on Oprah. Because bucket lists lack a *why*, you can accomplish everything and still be unfulfilled. Your goals have to be purposeful and mean something significant to you in order for you to be fulfilled by the process of accomplishing them and the outcome of completing them. An authentic heart-felt reason for pursuing a particular goal will yield more amazement and support than a goal that means a lot to everyone but you.

At work, most employees aren't clear on why they are doing certain tasks or projects. As a father of modern management, Peter Drucker once said, "There is nothing so useless as doing efficiently that which should not be done at all." It's usually not that certain tasks or projects don't have a *why*—it's usually assumed that the *why* is clear or nobody really knows why. For leaders, when the *why* isn't clear, people have to be managed and pushed using extrinsic motivation like money, the competition, a strong hand, and other incentives that ultimately don't increase engagement or improve results.

The number one reason goals don't get done right is because the purpose is not clear. I'm sure you've heard people mumble "Why are we doing this?" Instead of asking that question to the person who delegated the tasks to them, they do the work half-heartedly, which often yields poor or "just good enough" quality. If the purpose is clear, there are many ways to achieve a goal, but when it isn't clear there is only one right answer and that is whatever the boss wants.

Using the 8 Cylinders of Successful goal setting to clarify the *why* behind any goal, task, or project will ensure that everyone on your team is on the same page. Consider integrating Guaranteed Goals into your monthly meetings, internal business plans, and projects. If 30 days is too much time, simply shorten the time period without compromising the process, especially the *why* step.

THE 8 CYLINDERS OF SUCCESSFUL GOAL SETTING

Cylinder	Guiding Question	Unique Example Answer
Principles	What are my measurements for success on this goal? Do these measurements align with my measurements of success in life?	lbs. lost, decrease in caloric intake, how fast I can jog 3 miles
Passions	Will this allow me to directly use my passions? If not, can I integrate them in any way?	I can tie in my passion for cooking as I find new healthier recipes to prepare
Problem	Will this address a problem I have or care about?	My poor eating habits, low energy, and obesity in general
People	Will this allow me to serve myself better? Will this allow me to serve others better? Will this serve people I care about? Who am I doing this for?	My family, my colleagues, and me. Specifically, Me, John (husband), and Shannon (boss)
Positioning	Will this position me for my next step and future opportunities? Will this position me to be my best in this area?	chief financial officer in technology (though only correlative, most executives in my industry weigh less than me)
Pioneers	Will this challenge me to be someone I haven't been before? Will this challenge my status quo? Who do I know that has successfully done this before?	This will challenge my eating habits and force me to love myself like never before. Debbie (my best friend of 7 years)
Picture	Will this add color to the vision I have for myself? What will my life look like as I pursue this goal? What will change? How much time will I have to set aside every day or week to accomplish this?	travel to gym, 2 showers, work out, snacks, grocery store more often, Farmer's Market on the weekends, packing my lunch, additional $200/month and 10/hr/week commitment
Possibility	Will this create an impact that lasts beyond the goal? Will this open up new options for me that didn't exist before? Which ones? What will be possible in my life once I achieve this goal that wasn't possible before?	I will be able to live as the beautiful being that I know I am, I will have more time and energy to keep up with my kids and enjoy every day like never before

SAYING NO TO GOOD OPPORTUNITIES

Being clear on your *why* will also help you determine what you say "No" to. As someone who sets goals, you are probably already an inspiration to those around you in your personal life and at work, you're probably the one they give all of the extra work to. If you you want something done, give it to a busy person. Because of who you are, you have new opportunities coming at you left and right. **But the number one reason people's goals fail is that they say "Yes" to every good opportunity that comes their way rather than saying "No" to good opportunities so that they can be great at the great opportunities.**

Most of us consider ourselves to be busy. Each week, we all get 168 hours—no more, no less. Somehow, someway, we all filled up that space in time last week with sleep, work, travel, eating, talking, family, friends, and I don't know where the time went. **So whenever we set a new goal, the first question we have to answer before declaring a goal, is "What am I going to say 'No' to this week, that I did last week, to create space for my new goal?"**

Imagine that your life is a cup. And you can pour 168 hours of water into that cup. For most of us, our cup feels like it is already running over. Because we multi-task, we try to fit 200 hours worth of activity into a 168 hour cup. And along come your New Year's resolutions which each require time, attention, and energy and we try to pour all of those new goals onto (rather than into because there is no more space) a cup that is already full. Our new goals spill and then we say "New Year's resolutions don't work." The truth is that "I didn't do my work to identify what I was going to say 'No" to to make room for my New Year's resolutions."

SPILLING OVER VS. CREATING SPACE

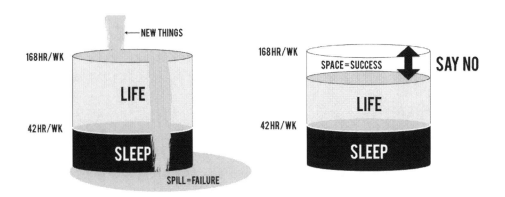

When you are clear on your *why* and your new goal is truly authentic, it will take priority over things you did last week. A goal is not just another to do list item to check off a list. It is a way of living and being that reflects our values through action. **When we change our being, our doing also changes.** Perhaps you have to give up unintentional TV time or social media to study for your entrance exam because your value helping others through your career. Or you wake up earlier to make time in the morning for exercise because your value health. Or you actually utilize your lunch break to write your book instead of working at your desk because your value your message. **If you don't create space for your goals in advance, they are bound to fail in the end.**

Good Execution of this Principle

"What for?"

Your goal is to run a marathon, but you're not one of those people who just does things to be able say that you did it. When friends ask you to join them, you reply "What for?" Plus, you know that there are all kinds of marathons for all kinds of causes all of the time. Raising money for the sake of it doesn't appeal to you either. You have a conversation with a friend that is considering adopting and the process intrigues you. You go on to do a little more research on your own and you are moved by what you find. You would run on behalf of foster kids, but there aren't any marathons for that in your area. So you set a date, make a flyer, send a couple of emails, and organize your own marathon at the local track and your raise money using PayPal just like the bigger marathons. You vow to create a college scholarship fund for foster youth in the area with the proceeds. Now you have a compelling reason to run, get in shape, and integrate your new passion.

Chapter 2

30 Days vs. 365 Days

"Work expands so as to fill the time available for its completion."

— *Cyril Northcote Parkinson*

Most people only evaluate themselves and their goals on New Year's Eve or on their birthday. One assumption with New Year's resolutions is that every resolution will take a year to complete. In fact, some of the goals that we set can be accomplished in a day, a week, or in a month. If someone says "I want to travel to this year," they can buy a plane ticket on January 1st and essentially be done. If someone else says "I want to start a business," they can go online and complete the incorporation process within a week. **365 days is an arbitrary number and has no significance to effective goal setting.** If something takes 365 days to complete, I would look at it as a big project with smaller sub-goals rather than a single goal. My fear is not that people set goals that are too big— it is that they set goals that are too small in relation to the time allotted for the goal.

365 days is too long. Most people don't even remember their New Year's resolutions by the end of January, let alone the end of the year. In 2002 researchers Norcross, Mrykalo and Blagys, of the University of Scranton, surveyed 159 New Year's resolvers and 123 nonresolvers who chose to wait until "later" to solve their problems. The two groups did not differ in terms of demographic characteristics, problem histories, or behavioral goals (weight loss, exercise program, and smoking cessation being the most prevalent). Resolvers reported higher rates of success than nonresolvers; at six

53

months, 46% of the resolvers were successful compared to 4% of the nonresolvers.

Considering that only 4% of nonresolvers accomplished their goals, it makes me wonder whose goals the nonresolvers are accomplishing if any at all. But the striking result about this research is that after only 6 months, 46% of resolvers New Year's resolutions were already complete, meaning many of their resolutions didn't require a full year to complete. In fact, most New Year's resolutions don't take a year to complete. One year is an arbitrary check point that someone chose and people agreed with. Besides changing the year on your checks and papers, there isn't much significance in the shift between December 31st and January 1st when it comes to goals.

BREAKING GOALS DOWN

So how often should we renew our goals? There is no direct answer, but 30 days establishes a nice cycle for any size goal, whether you are breaking a big goal into 12 smaller pieces or you are establishing one thing you want to accomplish over the next four weeks. We can gain some insight on how to break up our year by examining how people break up hours to maximize productivity and accuracy at work. There has been some research on break-taking and how often we should take them between periods of work. Researchers Balci and Aghazedeh of Louisiana State University tested 30 subjects to assess their data entry speed and accuracy using three work-rest schedules:
   » 60 minutes of work and 10 minutes of rest
   » 30 minutes of work and 5 minutes of rest
   » 15 minutes of work and 30 seconds of rest

They indicated that a work-rest schedule produced significant reductions in neck, shoulder, upper and lower back, chest and elbow/arm discomfort, eyestrain, blurred vision, as well as enhanced performance efficiency. According to Balci and Aghazedeh (2003), 15 minutes of work followed by a 30 second micro-break resulted significantly enhanced performance and lowered levels of discomfort.

WORK-REST RATIOS

Work-Rest Schedule	Work-Rest Ratio
60 minutes to 10 minutes	120:20 or 6:1
30 minutes to 5 minutes	60:10 or 6:1
15 minutes to 30 seconds	30:1

If you take the work-rest ratio for each of the schedules tested, you will see that the 15 minutes of work and 30 seconds of rest is equivalent to 30:1. When applied to the Guaranteed Goals, the result is 30 days to one day or 29 days of goal achievement for every one day of goal setting. Choosing when to renew, reset, and revitalize is key to your performance and success. Once a year is too long.

PARKINSON'S LAW

In corporate culture, every one is supposed to look busy. If someone doesn't look busy, it is perceived that they are not working hard. This culture of looking busy causes people to fill time and stretch out tasks. The employee who finishes their project in the first two days looks lazy whereas the employee who waits until the 29th day looks busy. This is known as Parkinson's Law, which suggests that "*Work expands so as to fill the time available for its completion."* If we have 30 days to complete a task that really only takes two days, we will likely take 30 days to do it. In essence, many companies are paying employees for 30 days of work but only two days of productivity.

In this information and technology-based economy, the 40 hour work week is dying. The moment you shift from hourly wages to salary, work has no boundaries. I know lawyers and bankers that work 80-100 hour weeks. In addition to working on weekends, they are given Blackberries by their companies, which allows them to be accessed at any time. Both my parents were doctors, and I used to hate when they were "on call". **In today's work world, a lot of people are on call at all times, but more time doesn't end procrastination or increase productivity—more time actually increases procrastination and decreases productivity.**

24 hour access does not lead to more productivity, or better results, except in extremely time sensitive businesses. Eight hours of 100% (8 hrs x 100% = 8 hrs) engagement is equivalent to 12 hours of only 67% (12 hrs x 67% = 8 hrs) engagement. If the work week stopped at 40 hours— meaning that the office doors open at 9am and lock at 6pm every weekday and we take away the Blackberries—I guarantee that an equal amount of work would get done. If we know that the amount of time that we have access to resources (colleagues, computers, clients) is limited, we will value them more and be more productive with the time that we do have. In the 60 hour versus 40 hour work week scenario above, employees could get 20 hours of their 168-hour week back and companies could lower their overhead by a significant amount.

There is no limit on the amount of work to do. However, there is a limit on one's ability to perform at their peak throughout the day. The eight hour work day may not even be the right number—in some countries, people work less than six hours a day. When we aren't maximizing our time at work, we tend to feel guilty and unproductive. I know that when I've dedicated a day to writing but I feel like I've wasted a morning, I tend to stay up late at night to make up for my earlier unproductivity. Whereas, if I know I have a meeting in the afternoon, I'm more productive in the morning because I know there is a hard stop at a particular time. **We have to put limits and boundaries on how long we work. When we do, we actually increase our productivity.**

What do you think would happen if you stood in the parking lot of any Fortune 500 company on a Friday afternoon and surveyed employees before they got in their cars by asking "What is the single most important thing you accomplished this week?" Most employees wouldn't have a good answer. Imagine starting each week with a goal setting meeting where each employee or team created a Guaranteed Goal for that week based on the company's strategy with an awareness that they would have to present their results to the entire company on Friday afternoon. A company could significantly increase its employees' productivity if Guaranteed Goals were set weekly. In addition to the company achieving better financial results if the goals are meaningful and properly chosen, employees would feel more valuable and significant because their accomplishments are being acknowledged and celebrated.

GOAL STACKING & SELF-MASTERY

At the beginning of the year, we tend to come up with a laundry list of new goals and that's part of the problem. We are trying to do too many new things at one time. In our effort to make sweeping changes in our lives, no change gets made at all.

If I challenged you to learn 5 languages at the same time you would be overwhelmed. But if I said master Spanish first, and then Mandarin, and then French, and then Portuguese, and then Swahili, you would have a greater chance of success. When you study how people master multiple languages or instruments, they didn't learn them all at the same time. They learned them one-by-one.

When you focus on one thing at a time and master it, three things happen:
1. You master the subject matter
2. You master the process of mastery
3. You master yourself

While some languages have similar words and structures, that's not where the advantage is in learning a second language. The real edge is in the 2nd and 3rd forms of mastery. Because you mastered the 1st language, you know what mastery requires and can apply that to the 2nd language which will accelerate how fast you learn it. And finally, because you've mastered yourself, you now know your learning style and what works best for you and can tailor your development accordingly.

This is why I believe in goal stacking. By goal stacking, I don't mean stacking on as many goals as you possibly can in the New Year. I actually mean the opposite. By goal stacking, I'm suggesting that you add on one goal at a time.

On January 1st, you may write down all of your goals for the year, but on January 2nd, I want you to only choose one to focus on for the month. Throughout January, you will have to say "No" to your old ways of being to create space for the new goal you want to do and you'll have a month to successfully integrate the new goal into your life before stacking on another one in February. By the end of January, the new rhythm of your life will feel familiar. Your mental capacity to take on a new goal will increase throughout the month because you won't have to think about going to the gym or writing daily—they will have become habit. Goal stacking gives you ample time to redesign your life piece-by-piece instead of trying to destroy and rebuild it in day.

Here is what a Guaranteed Goal stacked year looks like:

GUARANTEED GOAL	J	F	M	A	M	J	J	A	S	O	N	D
Host Monthly Goals Group	1	2	3	4	5	6	7	8	9	10	11	12
Earn & save $1K per month		1	2	3	4	5	6	7	8	9	10	11
Run marathon & Lose 30 lbs			1	2	3							
Grow a garden				1	2	3	4	5	6	7		
Meditate 15 minutes/day					1	2	3	4	5	6	7	8
Write my book in 6 months						1	2	3	4	5	6	
Blog 4x per month							1	2	3	4	5	6
Try 3 new dishes/month								1	2	3	4	5
Change jobs									1	2		
Donate $300/month										1	2	3
Write 8 thank yous/month											1	2
Read a book a month												1

I'm not saying that you should only "do" one goal at a time. I'm suggesting that you should only "start" one goal at a time. For example, in January, I may only focus on hosting a Guaranteed Goals group which I want to happen monthly throughout the year. If I succeed at goal #1 in January, in February I will add on my financial goal.

If you don't succeed at goal #1 in January, try again in February and push back all of your other goals one month because it's likely that you're not going to succeed at an additional goal if you didn't succeed at your January goal. And that process continues throughout the year.

Goal stacking also helps due to the fact that some goals are seasonal and some goals don't take all year. For instance, growing a garden can only happen during certain months of the year or writing a book may only take 6 months to do.

Good Execution of this Principle

"I need more time."

You have had an amazing idea for a book in your mind for years now, but you've haven't written anything. Every year you enthusiastically set a New Year's resolution to write your book by committing to one page per day. You get to page 10 and then life takes over and you default to "I need more time." This year it's going to be different. Though its January, and National Novel Writing Month isn't until November, you decide to create your own writing month. You invite a group of friends to join you and you make a pact to share complete first drafts in 30 days. To raise the stakes a little bit, everyone has to contribute $100 to a pot that is split among all of those who reach a certain page requirement.

---

Chapter 3

12 Small New Month's Resolutions vs. A Few Big New Year's Resolutions

"An optimist stays up until midnight to see the new year in. A pessimist stays up to make sure the old year leaves."

— Bill Vaughan

Instead of New Year's resolutions, I propose that we set New Month's Resolutions. I believe that you can get almost any goal or project well under way within 30 days. For instance, my first book, *The 8 Cylinders of Success,* took three years to write from page one to publication. I started writing and then I stopped and then I would start again. I didn't have a deadline or any accountability. **Accountability is the difference between goal setters and goal achievers.** When I truly evaluated how long it should take to write a book of this nature, I realized that 30 disciplined days was enough to get 80% of a book done. So I set a Guaranteed Goal or New Month Resolution to complete the first draft of this book in 30 days by emailing 150 of my friends and promising them that I would send them the first draft 30 days from the date of the original email.

Many people think that it is impossible to write a book. Some common excuses are "I can't sit down that long" or "I don't know if I have that much to say." It's more that possible and you don't even have to be a full-time professional writer to do so. A recent statistic showed that 3,000 books are being published every day. National Novel Writing Month is a 10-year-old movement that has inspired hundreds of thousands of writers to write a 175-page (50,000-word) novel between

November 1st and November 30th every year. In 2007, over 100,000 writers participated in the movement. Participants are encouraged to partner with other writers, and they are recognized on the organization's website (www.nanowrimo.org) if they meet the deadline.

You can use this same type of structure and look at every 30 Day Do It goal like a mini-competition between you and your best self to eventually align who you are with who you want to be. I think it's more powerful to accomplish 12 small projects sequentially than to try to accomplish a few major projects by the end of the year. Even if your big goal is to lose 120 pounds in a year, you can create 12 ten pound monthly goals instead of one big 120 pound goal.

When I was assigned my first major college paper, my professor told me to look at it like a big elephant stuck in a dorm room. The only way to get it out is piece-by-piece. Producing and consuming information in bite-size units is the best way to learn. I recently discovered that students at Cornell College in Iowa take one class at a time for three-and-a-half weeks, and then they get a four-day break before engaging a new subject. This schedule challenges the semester or quarter notion and suggests that students can focus and learn more on this type of academic calendar. They cover just as much material, but it is sequenced in a different way. It's easier to focus on one thing at a time than it is to multi-task. But we get so ambitious at the New Year that we set too many goals at once. Instead, we should focus on one worthwhile thing at a time, one month at a time.

DRIVING SCHOOL FOR LIFE GUARANTEED GOAL

My course and company, Driving School for Life and the Department of Motivated Vehicles grew out of a Guaranteed Goal. In November of 2008, I was writing the second draft of my book *The 8 Cylinders of Success* and I realized that in order to write the book, I needed to facilitate a course about it to see if it actually created value for people. The last thing I wanted to do was write a book just to say I wrote one. My intention was to write a book that transformed the lives of millions of people. So on November 10th, I sent out the email below for a test drive of my course on Saturday, November 22nd.

I sent the invitation to approximately 150 people and that caused 8 people to register. When I sent out the email, I did not have a curriculum in place. Essentially, I had 12 days to create a powerful nine hour experience based on *The 8 Cylinders of Success* to help people discover and align their lives with their purpose. This required creating a PowerPoint presentation, developing activities for each of the 8 principles, creating a workbook, printing, buying supplies, cleaning my house, and grocery shopping.

At the time, I was also working full-time—nonetheless I delivered. It wasn't perfect to say the least. In comparison to where the course is about a year later, it was about 80% right. About a month and a half later in January 2009, during the worst financial crisis of my lifetime, I quit my job to create my first company, The Department of Motivated Vehicles, and lead Driving School for Life course nationwide full-time. Since the first course, I have facilitated the course dozens of times across the country every month using Guaranteed Goals process to build momentum and a movement.

63

:: Driving School for Life ::

Driving School for Life is a personal development course I created in conjunction with my first book, which is currently being written. It documents the journey of three millennials as they participate in the 8 week course designed to help them gain clarity on their purpose and strengthen their friendship.

:: The Test Drive :: *A*

I am inviting 8 people to join me on Saturday, November 22nd from 9am-6pm to experience a simplified version of the 8 week curriculum. My intent is to learn from you and your experiences so that I can integrate themes that come from your stories into the actual book to make it more powerful and transformational.

Participants will:

» Get a chance to meet 8 other incredible people
» Clarity on your life's direction as we approach 2009
» FREE breakfast and lunch
» Get a free signed copy of the book when it is published

:: The 8 Hours of Power ::

The 8 Hours of Power are based on the 8 Cylinders of Success, which include: your principles, passions, problems, people, picture, pioneers, positioning, and possibility. Each principle will have interactive activities and discussions to draw out the best in you.

:: Date & Location ::

Saturday, November 22nd from 9am-6pm
1000 Some Place Avenue, Some City

:: RSVP ::

Please email if you are interesting in participating. If you can't participate, please forward this email to anyone you think may benefit from and add value to this space.

Thank you for supporting me on my journey!

Had it not been for me creating that initial Guaranteed Goal, I would not be where I am today as an author, speaker, consultant, and coach as quickly as I have gotten here. I attribute my success today to that single email through which I made a no-turning-back decision about the direction of my life.

Now I use this process in all areas of my life, with my coaching clients, and the students of my courses. All of this and more is possible in your life using Guaranteed Goals and Guaranteed Goals Groups to your advantage. I want to put an end to the concept of the New Year's resolution by introducing the New Month's resolution.

The Proof Is In The Pudding
Picture of the November 22, 2008 Driving School For Life Group

REPURPOSING PROCRASTINATION

I've already demonstrated that shorter more frequent breaks can increase performance, but regardless of how frequent breaks are, procrastination will likely still be present. *The nature of procrastination: A meta-analytic and theoretical review of quintessential self-regulatory failure* by Piers Steel, a research at the University of Calgary, stated that an estimated 80–95%of students have problems with procrastination and 15-20% of adults identify as procrastinators. He cites many potential causes of procrastination including task characteristics, timing of rewards and punishment, task aversiveness, neuroticism, among others. Since procrastination is so present in our lives, we should learn how to use it to our advantage.

Dan Ariely and Klaus Wertenbroch of MIT and INSEAD conducted a study where they divided their students into three groups—evenly-spaced deadlines, self-imposed deadlines, and end deadlines—to proofread papers. Students were rewarded for every error they found and penalized for tardiness. The evenly-spaced group, which submitted one paper every 7 days, detected more errors, had fewer delays in submissions, and had the highest average earnings. We currently space our goals out by years, but perhaps evenly-spaced monthly goals that build to a larger goal is a more powerful way toward goal achievement.

Guaranteed Goals suggests that we adopt the concept of New Month's resolutions instead of New Year's resolutions. Guaranteed Goal Setting doesn't stop procrastination, but it structures deadlines (i.e. every third Thursday) to improve your performance, punctuality, and progress. The way to fight procrastination is to break big tasks into smaller tasks and create deadlines for the smaller tasks. You will probably still procrastinate on the smaller task, but you will finish ahead of the real deadline.

FINDING FLOW

Procrastination and perfectionism usually have to do with the fear of being judged because we have difficulty separating how we perform from who we are. A goal's outcome speaks mostly to your external performance. Once the goal is actually complete you are able to receive accurate feedback on your performance. What you learn about yourself as a person will come mostly from internal insights during the journey, and especially around completion time. Since purposeful goals should be unique to you, the journey may be alone, meaning that only you will be able to honestly evaluate your process.

Immediate feedback is one of the key criteria in achieving a flow in life. Psychologist Mihaly Csikzentmihalyi defines flow as a state of concentration or complete absorption with the activity at hand and the situation. His research shows that there are three conditions of flow experiences:

» A person faces a clear set of goals that require appropriate responses
» Immediate feedback is provided
» A person's skills are fully involved in overcoming a challenge that is just about manageable

When these three conditions are in place, attention becomes fully invested in accomplishing the goal at hand. He argues that "it is the full involvement of flow, rather than happiness, that makes for excellence in life." Unfortunately only 20% of people have been involved in something so deeply that nothing else seems to matter.

Guaranteed Goals will help you establish the conditions for flow by clarifying what your goal looks like when you are finished and you celebrate through your presentation to a small group. The frequency of monthly gatherings will give you feedback on your performance, which is more than you're probably getting anywhere now. And finally, your group or accountability system will push you to create challenging goals that truly test your skills and cause you to grow.

Good Execution of this Principle

"I don't know where to begin."

You can't stand microwave dinners and eating out is getting expensive, but you don't know how to cook. Learning to cook has been on your list of goals for years but you always say "I don't know where to begin". The only way to learn to cook is to do it. So this year, you decide to host a potluck dinner at your home once a month. In January, you send out all 12 dates for the entire year, and each month you ask one of your friends who can cook to co-host it with you and you invite them to come prepare the main course at your home so that you can learn from them. Over a 12 month period, you learn 12 new recipes and 12 new cooking styles so that you can start experimenting on your own.

ACCOUNTABILITY:
Create Positive
Peer Pressure

Chapter 4

Event-Based vs. Date-Based

"The best way to predict the future is to create it."
— Divine Bradley

One of the primary reasons we set goals is to learn about ourselves through the goal achievement process—it isn't always just to get something done. Goals are tests we create to explore what we're really capable of. **A goal is a possibility someone creates for himself or herself and as the opening quote of the chapter says "The best way to predict the future is to create it."**

Most people think that the future comes when it comes, when in reality, the future lies in the present moment. Anything on your calendar beyond this moment is a future you created. **And the more people that you can get to believe in that future with you, the more likely it is that it will become real. If you don't create your future, other people will, including your employer, parents, other companies, and more.**

Event-based goals are driven by more external factors than date-based goals. When a goal leads up to an event that involves other people and some sort of presentation by the goal setter, the likelihood of its completion is greater than a goal that is only driven by a date. **A date without consequences (i.e. financial loss, light-hearted embarrassment) for poor performance is not an accountability mechanism**. Obviously, events involve a date, but date-based goals can easily be pushed back, whereas event-based goals push you to finish because they involve other people.

Traditional goal setting, as mentioned in the introduction, suggests that once you think of a goal, the next step is to set a due date for when you want to complete that goal. When this is the case, due dates can keep getting extended for days, weeks, months, or even years. After that, the next step is to create a plan to complete the goal. The goal is broken down into small steps, which manifest as a plan of action or a to-do list. Many people don't even get this far.

Self-Imposed Deadlines

The person who assesses their ability appropriately and only needs two days to complete the goal could have easily finished by day two, but there are a few reasons that prevent us from accomplishing our goals before the imposed deadline. Some people believe that they work better under pressure. In reality, the goal was probably too easy to begin with and time was a factor that they could control by lessening it to make the goal more challenging. Other people like to feel busy—they always like having unchecked boxes on their to-do list as much as they like checking things off of it. This is often due to our desire to want to know what to do next as well as our fear of not knowing what to do with ourselves if we were to finish early.

On the other hand, when you finish early, you may deal with perfectionism. Because there's so much time left you may continue to iterate, edit, or revise and not know when to stop. By the 30 day mark you may have done the goal three times over and still feel as if it's not perfect. If this is you, I would recommend shortening your Guaranteed Goal to 14 days and being satisfied with whatever you have at that time, even if you have 14 more days to deliver. I would even go as far as presenting or submitting early after revisions to get the project off of your mind and create mental space for new goals and projects.

Creating change in your life and the lives of others is 20% planning and 80% execution. The process of sending out an invitation, creating a to-do list, and planning a simple celebration should require no more than 20% of your energy. Keep in mind that the invitation step comes first, not last. The only thing you have to do to set the celebration in motion is send out invitations to people that matter including friends, family, mentors, or colleagues. Invitations should be sent out immediately after the goal is set to signify the you are committed. Since this simple step increases commitment so much, it really makes you assess *why* you chose the goal before you invest any more thought or physical energy.

The other 80% should be dedicated to achieving the goal. After the invitation is sent, it's up to the you to create a plan of action to achieve the goal and deliver for the celebration. At this point, you can procrastinate all you want as long as you achieve the goal by the event. If you know that a particular task will only take you two days to complete and you have 30 days to do it and you wait until the 29th day to begin, that is not procrastination. On the contrary, this is actually an example of great time management. It would only qualify as procrastination if you waited until the 29th day and realized that it would actually take you four days to achieve the goal at the level of quality you desired.

COLLECTIVE ACCOUNTABILITY

Alcoholics Anonymous (AA) is a mutual-help (not self-help) organization to help anyone with the desire to overcome alcoholism recover. It has thousands of groups that meet everyday worldwide, and it has changed the lives of over two million people. The power of AA is in the collective accountability and positive expectations environment they create through their daily support groups and sponsorships. At some meetings, members introduce themselves by sharing their name and how many days they have been sober. After being sober for a while, older members start sponsoring new members. When you know that the person you are sponsoring expects you to be sober in order to help them stay sober, your commitment to sobriety increases.

There are countless studies that confirm that formal treatment in addition to AA's mutual-support structure successfully promotes abstinence from alcohol and other drugs better than formal treatment alone. Timko, Moss, Finnery, and Lesar (2000) compared the one-year and three-year abstinence rates of people with formal treatment only and formal treat with AA. They discovered that people who only did formal treatment only had a 20.6% one-year abstinence rate and a 25.9% three-year abstinence rate, whereas people who did formal treatment with AA had a 42.4% one-year abstinence rate and 50.9% three-year abstinence rate. Participating in AA meetings nearly doubled abstinence rates.

This study and others reveal the power of having a consistent ongoing community to keep you accountable to your own commitments. To only set goals at the New Year and then never reconnect with those whom you set goals is like going to formal treatment only. **We can achieve more together through creating simple check points along the way.**

Good Execution of this Principle

"See you soon."

Your goal this year is to spend more time with family and friends. You're tired of not seeing the people you love as often as you would like. In the past, work seemed to fill up every empty moment you had. So this year, instead of leaving their presence and not knowing when you are going to see your parents, siblings, or best friends next, you decide to plan out some fun events throughout the year (i.e. picnics, sports games, laser tag, the zoo, camping, etc.) so that you always have a date and idea in mind for your next outing before you meet up with them. Just before you separate, you joyfully invite them to your next event in person and you follow up immediately with an email or text message before either of you drives off via your phone. It's not perfect, but it is a lot better than saying "See you soon."

Chapter 5

Celebrate On vs. Celebrate If

"Celebrating creates an atmosphere of recognition and positive energy. Imagine a team winning the World Series without champagne spraying everywhere. And yet companies win all the time and let it go without so much as a high five. Work is too much a part of life not to recognize moments of achievement. Make a big deal out of them. If you don't, no one will."

— Jack Welch

Guaranteed Goal Setting begins with the celebration. Instead of saying, "I'm going to complete my certification *by* January 1st," Guaranteed Goals require that you say "*on* January 1st" because setting your celebration in motion is one of the initial steps of the process. Most New Year's resolutions are forgotten by the end of January. If the proper accountability structures are not set when the goal is set, then the likelihood that the goal is achieved will be low.

With traditional goal setting, celebration and incentives are contingent on the goal being achieved. In our personal lives, we make statements like, "If I lose 25 pounds I will take myself on vacation." In our professional lives, bonus structures may be set up based on reaching certain sales goals and quotas. A Guaranteed Goal celebration is created with the belief that the goal will be achieved. The celebration is simply a space for you to share your results with those who care about you and are holding you accountable. By beginning with the planning of the celebration, the you knows that at some particular date you will have to present yourself and your work in front of friends, family, and other supporters. Therefore, the celebration serves as an accountability structure and an affirmation of you.

As Jack Welch, General Electric's most celebrated CEO, articulated in the opening quote of the chapter, celebration is the most underrated part of leadership and goal setting. We set goals as individuals and organizations, but then we don't celebrate when we achieve them. Instead, we get somewhere and want more. It's okay to want more, but first acknowledge how far you've come. Celebration is only unwarranted when the goal was too low in the first place. If you want to be a millionaire, plan a celebration once you reach it and then set a new goal during or after the celebration. **Without celebration, goal achievement becomes a never-ending race and the goal setter feels incomplete and there is always more to do.**

Celebration can be a simple self or public recognition that you achieved something you said you would and upheld a commitment to yourself and others. The celebration doesn't have to be extravagant. It's simply a set time and space that cannot be moved or canceled, where you know that you will have to deliver whatever you have at that time. Results should be given in person via a short presentation with supporting documents (i.e. papers, pictures, signed contracts, proposals, numbers, etc.) to verify that the goal was accomplished, followed by a space for feedback.

The Guaranteed Goal is designed to harness the energy required to get a majority of the work done. From there, you can iterate, edit, adjust, or revise. If the goal setter or team did not get feedback during the 30 days, then it should be assumed that the deliverable will only be 80% correct. Knowing that it only has to be 80% right (though 100% done) gives the goal setter the freedom to take risks, and the feedback givers the freedom to authentically critique, which will ultimately lead to the best results. We waste energy when we try to get everything 100% right the first time because it's often only 80% right anyway. The final 20% will be address during the feedback and iteration part of the process. The expectation for Guaranteed Goals should not be perfection—it should be quality results that match what the goal setter set out to achieve with room for feedback and improvement.

THE LAW OF EXPECTATIONS

The ability to shape your future for yourself and in the minds of others is called the Law of Expectations. The Law of Expectations states that whatever you expect and believe, whether this is positive or negative, becomes your reality. When one believes that good things will happen, they usually will. If one expects bad things to happen, then bad things will tend to happen. What's interesting about the Law of Expectations is that other people's expectations can affect the performance of an individual as well.

In 1992, Rosenthal, Robert & Jacobson, Lenore released a study called the *Pygmalion in the Classroom* to test the effect of one's expectations on the behavior of another. Teachers were told in advance that certain students were extremely bright and expected to make huge strides in their academic performance in the coming year. The teachers didn't know that the "bright" students were randomly selected, but because they believed that the students were exceptional, the students performed at much higher levels than their classmates. In essence, the teacher's expectations of the students became a self-fulfilling prophecy.

By creating the celebration in advance, Guaranteed Goals use the Law of Expectations to your advantage. In addition to you expecting to celebrate, everyone you invite has the expectation as well. Whereas in the *Pygmalion in the Classroom* only the teacher had the high expectation, Guaranteed Goals instills high expectations in you and your invitees. If you invite three people to your celebration, they will essentially create a three-teacher effect via invitations to add on to your own expectations of yourself once the invitations are sent.

Good Execution of this Principle

"I don't have time."

Your goal is to lose a significant amount of weight, but you claim "I don't have time." Despite your ambitious goal the year before, you gained more weight last year. Something has to change. You know that there are other people in your church community that want to lose weight too, but there aren't any ministries for physical health, only spiritual. So you approach the minister to share your weight *release* story for 5 minutes ever first Sunday of the month until you reach your goal to inspire health and wellness among all the members of the congregation. The minister agrees and since Sunday's not moving, you better get moving!

Chapter 6

Public & Peers vs. Private & Personal

"Again, I tell you that if two of you on earth agree about anything you ask for, it will be done for you by my Father in heaven. For where two or three come together in my name, there am I with them."

— Matthew 18:19-20

When it comes to personal goal setting, there are usually three parties involved—Me, Myself, and I. This is the worst checks and balances system ever. We write down our goals or try to remember them, but then we don't tell anyone else what they are. As a result, Me, Myself, and I try to hold each other accountable and end up pointing fingers at each other.

The legal system address this dilemma through lawyers or notary services. A notary is a third-party public officer constituted by law to verify and approve legal documents such as estates and deeds. By co-signing certain documents, they confirm that you are who you say you are, so that when the documents need to be used to make something happen, they can be trusted as truth. With at least three people involved, any agreement stands in a court of law.

Similarly, Guaranteed Goal Setting requires you to get others to sign off on your specific goals. Instead of sharing the goal as this huge draining thing to accomplish, the event invitation creates the expectation in their minds that the goal will be accomplished and all they have to do is come celebrate with you. **Without even knowing it, they are holding you accountable by committing to your celebration.** By simply accepting the invitation to your celebration your guest serve as an additional source of accountability. Now the goal is out of your head and into the world. Me, Myself, and I can relax and you can get going on your goals.

CREATING SUPPORT STRUCTURES

Amway is a direct selling company and manufacturer that uses multi-level marketing to sell a wide variety of products, primarily in the health and beauty industry. In 2008, they earned revenues of $8.2B. Rather than being given pre-established or printed goals by a manager, sales team members are required to set and write their own goals regularly. By writing down their own goals, team members feel more ownership and commitment to their goals which has resulted in higher sales for Amway.

The effectiveness of this internally-driven strategy can also work externally with customers. When selling products door-to-door, whether they are encyclopedias, Girl Scout cookies pre-orders, or vacuum cleaners, it seems like it would be courteous and convenient to write for the customer to make the sales process flow. Companies that sell products in this way have discovered that though the sales process may flow faster this way, so do returns and refunds. In order to change this pattern, sales team members simply started having the customer complete the sales contract in their own handwriting, and the result was less returns.

How can we apply this sales technique to goal setting? Dr. Gail Matthews of Dominican University studied how various combinations of commitments, reports, and friends supported the achievement of goals. The 149 students she studied were divided into 5 groups with varying levels of upfront commitment:

Group 1: Just think about your goals
Group 2: Just write your goals
Group 3: Write your goals and formulate action commitments
Group 4: Write your goals, formulate action commitments, and send them to a supportive friend
Group 5: Write your goals, formulate action commitments, do weekly progress reports, and send all three to a supportive friend

Members of group 5 achieved significantly more than any other group and members of group 1 achieve significantly less than any group that was required to write down their goals. This study provides empirical evidence for the effectiveness of three coaching tools: accountability, commitment and writing down one's goals. Guaranteed Goals and Guaranteed Goals Groups incorporate all of these support structures into the process. You may not need this particular combination of support structures, but you need to find what works for you.

A fitting proverb from an anonymous source reads, "The word that is heard perishes, but the letter that is written remains." In the cited research, the supportive friend writes in their calendar when they have to hold you accountable. In the same way, with Guaranteed Goals, your invitees write in their calendars the date of your celebration, demonstration, or presentation. In a sense, your goals create a ripple effect of goals and it is just as important for supportive friends to write down their goal to hold you accountable as it is for you to write down your goals. By doing so, you create your future in your mind and theirs.

POSITIVE PEER PRESSURE

There is a myth in the world that personal development is personal. I believe otherwise. If we could do things on our own we would have already done them. The people around us are the best form of accountability that we can have since we interact with them so frequently. The motivation that you get from reading a self-help book or going to a weekend conference is very difficult to sustain long-term without a supportive community.

Peer pressure has a connotation of being negative. The term conjures up thoughts of high schoolers urging their peers to drink alcohol or smoke against their will. This same force that encourages someone to do something that they don't want to do can also be used to encourage you to accomplish your goals. *Positive* peer pressure is a key component to Guaranteed Goals because it creates accountability without requiring any extra effort from peers beyond being a good friend.

We tend to put the goals of our spouse, children, boss, professors, and others ahead of our own. It's usually because we care about those people deeply. But how can you authentically encourage others to pursue their goals and dreams while not pursuing your own? Sometimes you have to be selfish and go after what you want. **We're more comfortable disappointing ourselves, than we are disappointing others.** However, you can use this innate desire to please others to your advantage if you can find others who are willing to help you, and hold you accountable in the same way you hold them accountable. Rather than looking at people-pleasing or caring what others think negatively, how can we use it to our advantage? We can simply leverage this desire to please others by getting those we love involved in our goals.

Our personal transformation also affects others. If other people are going to benefit from your growth, why not get them involved in holding you accountable to your goals. To take it one step further, there may be people already around you who would benefit from starting a Guaranteed Goals Group with you or doing a particular goal with you. Collaborative goal achievement has been proven to lead to better outcomes. Organizations like Alcoholics Anonymous, Weight Watchers, and Toast Masters have demonstrated the power of the collective. Marathon training groups are also great examples of individuals coming together to support one another in pursuit of a common goal.

WORD IS BOND

Accountability to your goals is a prerequisite for success and community accountability is one of the best ways to get it. Besides, accomplishing goals with friends involved is more fun anyway. When we commit to things publicly, we tend to do them lovingly or begrudgingly. "Word is bond" is a phrase that some people use as a form of promise because nobody likes to go back on their word. We want to appear consistent with our words and actions at all times to uphold our integrity in our own eyes and the eyes of others.

When it comes to personal affairs, we undervalue accountability, but in business affairs it is mandated. Every three months, public companies have to submit a report to the U.S. Securities and Exchange Commission, audited by professional accounts evaluating their financial performance. What's powerful about this system is that the SEC forces public companies to evaluate themselves at regular intervals. **In the same way that companies have to get external *accountants* to audit their financial health, we need *account-ability* partners who will make us *account* for all of the ability and potential within us!**

The reason we need accountability is because self-discipline is so rare. Discipline is so valuable nowadays that companies are able to build extremely profitable businesses around it. Some SAT, GRE, GMAT, LSAT, and MCAT preparation classes are able to charge more than $2,000 a piece to provide the test taker with assistance. However, the core value of these courses is in the discipline and structure they offer. The tricks and tips they give test takers aren't secrets and can be found in books published by the same company for $25.

PUBLIC RECOGNITION

In 1980, researchers Pallack, Cook, and Sullivan conducted a study in Iowa on how future public recognition might influence homeowners' conservation of energy. Initially, a researcher called in the middle of winter offering tips on how to conserve energy and save fuel. Though most people agreed verbally, no real savings accrued at the end of the month. Realizing that this strategy wasn't going to curb high-energy use, they chose to alter the experiment by promising to publish the family names of those who agreed to saving energy in a public newspaper article that honored them as public-spirited, fuel-conserving citizens.

The dial turned. At the end of the month, the utility company checked the meters and discovered that the families who agreed to saving energy with the promise of being honored publicly saved an average of 422 cubic feet of natural gas. This was a 12.2% gas savings during a season where energy demand is high and costly. To take the experiment even further, the researcher called back everyone after the first month and told them that their names couldn't be published after all to see what would happen. Strikingly, the families *increased* their energy savings to 15.5% for the remainder of the winter season. What happened? Ultimately, the homeowners knew and believed that it was good to save energy, but they never had a clear *why*. After changing their habits, saving energy and money, and realizing that it wasn't that hard, they didn't need the incentive to continue saving. The public recognition ended up just a catalyst to get them to change. Sometimes a kick start is all you need to change something forever.

Even before figuring out how to accomplish a certain goal, the best way to invest your thought energy is determining how to demonstrate that you've accomplished your goal and set a date for when you intend to celebrate it. In the energy saving experiment, the public recognition was created for the homeowners by the electric company, but you can create this for yourself with each of your monthly goals. You can arrange a celebration, presentation, or demonstration that involves the eyes of other people similar to the function of the newspaper article with family names. For example, someone who wants to be a better public speaker may choose to deliver a speech to a group of friends to demonstrate how they have improved through a month of disciplined practice. Or a person committed to working out may run a marathon in a certain time frame and invite their friends to the finish line to demonstrate that they are healthier. The celebration is not the goal—it is an accountability space setup by you to self-motivate and demonstrate to others that you've already accomplished the larger goal.

Most people think that simply setting deadlines is enough to inspire themselves and others to move and get things done, and that's why most goals are D.O.A. (Dead On Arrival). Dead-lines are lethal. What a terrible word and what a bad way to motivate yourself or other people! Deadlines *wire* instead of *inspire* people, taking away the enjoyment and creative energy that the goal setting process offers. If you miss this, you're dead!

87

Instead of deadlines, Guaranteed Goals uses headlines by encouraging you to activate your celebration up front instead of at the end. In the news, headlines are the cover story. In live performances, the headliner refers to the main event. Imagine being told that you are headlining next month's meeting—meaning that you will be the featured presentation. You are going to deliver! **Headlines are a lot more uplifting than deadlines because they encourage the best in others rather than discourage failure like deadlines.** Your Guaranteed Goal celebration should be a front-page worthy event that motivates you to do great and for others to be involved in your greatness.

Good Execution of this Principle

"I forgot."

Normally you would set New Year's resolutions with your friends and everyone would write their own goals on their own sheet of paper. In the past, that hasn't resulted in success for everyone. Everyone's excuse is "I forgot what my goals were." Even though you all set goals together, nobody knew each other's goals. So this year, you decide to bring butcher paper to the party and everyone is going to write down every else's goals. This year, success will be defined as how many goals you collectively cross off. Each time someone accomplishes a goal, everyone gets a phone call, text message, or email to cross it off of their butcher paper. In addition, every time you see each other is an opportunity to hold each other accountable.

ACTIVATION:
Find The First Domino & Burn The Boats

Chapter 7

The First Domino vs. Chronological Order

"A journey of a thousand miles must begin with a single step."

— Lao Tzu

The first step is always the biggest step—whether it's going to the gym for the first time in three years, opening that first box in the garage to see what you can throw away, donate, or sell, or registering for a certification course you need to advance professionally. When we set goals, they tend to be huge—we aren't inspired by small goals. No matter how big the goal is, the most important thing one can do is just start. Economist Vilfred Pareto created a concept called the 80-20 rule that states that, for many events, roughly 80% of the effects come from 20% of the causes. If you apply this to your goals, you don't have to think about the whole goal—that's overwhelming. Instead, you can look for the 20% that is significant and begin moving on that portion.

I call it finding the first domino. People set up dominoes in a way that when knocked down, the first domino causes all of the other ones to fall in sequence, hence the *domino effect*. We can instill the same effect to our goals by finding the first and simplest action that will automatically set the next actions in motion. After you've created your goal and the to-do list to achieve it, ask yourself, "What's the most significant thing I can do to set the goal in motion that will require the least amount of effort?" **The best way to accomplish goals isn't always in chronological order—it's to get started and this requires finding the easiest thing to do now.**

In primary school, I remember loving the teachers who allowed us to start our homework in class. Even if there were only 5 minutes left in the period and I only got two of the 30 problems done, I felt better about the rest of the assignment. As with goals, there were three types of students:

Student #1: Those who didn't write the homework down or utilize the 5 minutes

Student #2: Those who wrote it down but packed up their bag and just sat there, and

Student #3: Those who wrote it down and started the assignment

I would argue that those who started had a higher completion rate than the other two groups, but their choice may be attributed to a lot of other factors. I would also argue that despite these unknown factors, if the teacher required all students to complete the first two questions before they left alone or in groups, the completion rate would rise significantly.

As discussed in the section on physics, an object set in motion tends to stay in motion, unless a counter force pushes against it. Usually that counter force is everyday life. **Since most new goals aren't integrated into our everyday life when we set them, we have to make room for them first or else they will end up last.** Goals that endure become habits, which involve an inner lifestyle change that affects your beliefs an attitudes. Ultimately, these changes begin effecting your external choices, routines, and rhythms.

FIGHTING FEAR & FAILURE

Fear of failure is probably the number one factor that prevents people from even starting their goals. Any goal you set is going to take you to a new place inside of yourself and the world and fear of the unknown is natural. **But it isn't that fearless people have no fear, it's that the desire to accomplish the goal is stronger than the fear they possess.** We can do simple things that change the nature of our fear instantaneously.

The ancient Greek army's war strategy best demonstrated the fight through fear. When they traveled across the Mediterranean to do battle, the first thing they did when they arrived was burn their boats. With their escape route gone, they had two choices—win or die. I think it is evident what they chose. With the simple strike of a match, the tables turned and fear became a motivator instead of a demotivator. The match is similar to the first domino—it's easy to initiate and it sets everything else in motion. It signifies the point of no return to your former self.

Excuses and escape routes are our boats—they offer alternatives to facing the future that we claim we want. Our goals are our intentions, but without a fight, there can be no victory. If you have a goal, but are afraid to commit, force yourself into action by burning the boats. Register for an exam in advance if you want to go back to school. Buy a plane ticket to move to a new city before even signing a lease. **Fear of failure disappears when you realize it can't save you. The way to succeed is to fail at something big. Failure is simply success at something you didn't intend to achieve while success is achieving what you intended.** When you authentically go after goals that seem impossible, you tend to succeed at amazing things you wouldn't have imagined if you didn't attempt the goal at all.

GOAL ACTIVATION

Everyone talks about goal setting, but nobody focuses on goal achievement. Every year, individuals take a day to set goals and then forget about them and companies lay out strategic goals but don't activate them. The most important and most forgotten part of the goal setting process is the activation phase. To activate something simply means to start it. We all deal with individual inertia—a comfort with things being the way they are. Since most goals are added onto life instead of integrated in to our everyday life when we set them, we have to make room for them first or else they will end up lost on our to-do lists. The difficulty of the integration process is one of the key reasons Guaranteed Goal Setting suggests that you should only activate one goal every 30 days.

In life, there are millions of decisions to make, but usually there are only two choices: yes or no. Most goals don't get accomplished because people aren't willing to say "yes" or "no" to the habits required to achieve them. Since getting the goal underway is so important, the key is to find out what you are willing to say "yes" to among all of the things on your to-do list. Some people call this "the lowest hanging fruit" and salesmen call it "low-balling". Low-balling is a persuasive technique that works by first gaining commitment to an idea or item at a lower cost than you really intend to charge, then, using the fact that people will behave consistently with their earlier commitments even if you change the agreement.

Cialdini, Cacioppo, Bassett, and Miller demonstrated the effectiveness of low-balling by asking students to participate in an unpleasant early morning experiment. They called one sample and asked them to participate in the 7am "thinking process." Only 24% of those called agreed. They used the low-ball technique on the second sample by asking them if they were willing to participate first *and then* letting them know the time. 56% of the second sample said they were willing to participate. None of them changed their mind after hearing the time, and all of them showed up at 7am!

Though low-balling may be manipulative when used on others, it can be extremely effective when used on self. Similar to the experiment, one of the keys to Guaranteed Goal Setting is identifying your activator. **Your activator is that low-time, low-energy, low-cost action item that you will say "yes" to before concluding the goal setting process and trying to move onto the goal-achievement process.** Remember, one of the best activators is sending out an invitation to your demonstration, celebration, or presentation. It requires very little time, no money, no people, and it's easy. Below is an example of an "I Choose List" and how to find your "activator item" for the first draft of a book.

An "I Choose List" is for you by you. To-do lists are for your work and other demands of life and are usually determined by someone else. Your "I choose list" is all about what you are committed to regardless of what others think and want you to do. After setting your goal, you can work backwards to determine your "I Choose List" items that will get you there (column 1). From there, you can put in rough estimates fro time, money, people, and ease. Finally, you can look for the activator item and create an order for your goal achievement.

I CHOOSE LIST—WRITING A BOOK IN 30 DAYS

1. Action Item	2. Time	3. Money	4. People	5. Ease	6. Order	Chron-illogical
Mind map chapters	3 hrs	$0	me	medium	2	1
Trademark theory	30 min	$275	lawyer	easy	3	6
Copyright #1	30 min	$35	lawyer	easy	6	5
Write book	30 days	$0	me	hard	4	2
Find an editor	2 hrs	$1005	editor	medium	5	3
Send invitations	30 min	$0	me	easy	1st domino	7
Celebrate 1st draft	3 hrs	$50	friends	easy	7	4

In this case, the activator is sending invitations—it's the shortest, lowest cost, easiest, and only requires me. Setting the celebration in motion marries the goal setting and goal achievement stages together. Thus momentum keeps building. Most people would send invitations after the first draft was written, but by sending it first, you create accountability for yourself. Oftentimes we try to handle to-do lists that will get us through the goal-achievement stage in chronological order. In this case, that means that mind mapping the chapters would have probably been first.

Success has a sequence and it's usually not in the order our mind thinks it is. Chron-illogical order will leave you stuck at ground zero focusing on the hardest most difficult thing. Guaranteed Goals changes that by having you identify and place the activator item first.

JUST TIE YOUR SHOES FIRST

I remember when we had a bad winter in New York. Prior to that, I rode my bike to my office for fun and for exercise. But once the first snow hit, it didn't let up until March. So, I started working from home. That also meant I wasn't exercising daily and I started to feel it in my body. I asked my wife if we could get an exercise bike so that I could start my morning routine again despite the weather. She said "Yes."

It arrived, I put it together, and I placed it in the room next to our bedroom. I went to sleep that night excited to ride my new bike in the morning. I woke up the next morning and sure enough, I didn't even touch the bike. Throughout the remainder of the day and the week, I avoid that room entirely.

What happened? My original (valid) excuse about the bad weather was was gone and yet I ended up replacing that excuse with more excuses. I'm too busy. I didn't want to wake you up. I need to eat first. I don't want to stink up the house. It's not the same as riding a real bike because it's stationary. I don't want to change clothes if I'm working from home. I just showered last night and I don't want to waste water. Those excuses weren't real. The thought of getting on the bike for 30 minutes was honestly daunting—especially when I didn't feel I was physically going anywhere.

After awhile, I ran out of excuses and I had to face the truth and that's when it hit me. I had to find the first domino and I found it in an unexpected place. When I initially broke down all of the steps it takes to get from out of my bed onto the exercise bike, it felt a little elementary.

1. Get out of bed
2. Take off your night wear
3. Put on your exercise clothes
4. Put on your shoes
5. Drink a glass of water
6. Walk to the other room
7. Start your playlist
8. Get on the bike
9. Start pedaling
10. Keep going for 30 minutes

Normally I woke up focused on step 10 which was the hardest part of all and repelled me the most. Instead I started focusing on simply tying my shoes. And guess what? I found that once I tied my shoes, I had a 100% chance of getting on the bike. If a kindergartener can tie their shoes, so can I. So now I wake up and focus on tying my shoes. And guess where I put my shoes in the morning? Right beside my bed. For me, tying my shoes was the first domino—it was the easy trigger that got me over the hump of my laziness.

Good Execution of this Principle

"Someday."

You've always wanted to travel the world, but you always have a good excuse why you can't, so "someday" is a common word in your vocabulary. And then an email from an airline company gets forwarded to you by four of your friends who are aware of your goal and the subject say "$2,000 for UNLIMITED flights for a month." Work is heavier than it has ever been but you haven't even used your vacation days for the past 2 years. This is a once and a lifetime opportunity and you have the savings to handle the costs. In most cases you would try to plan everything out before making a commitment, but as someone who has already priced out a global trip at almost five-figures, you know you can't beat this deal. You only have two options. Press purchase and trust that everything else will fall into place or pass. Click!

Chapter 8

Input-focused vs. Outcomes-focused

"The longest journey of any person is the journey inward."

— *Dag Hammarskjold*

In today's society, we tend to value the product over the process, the award over the effort, and the incentives over the investment. Incentives and awards are short-lived; nonetheless, we value the championship trophy more than we value the road that leads there. We value the promotion more than we value the experiences and lessons that cause it. Outcomes are great, but if it's true that you get of out of life what you put into it, then we should primarily focus on input or effort since that's all we really have control over.

Each goal you set should pull you closer towards your highest self. The essential question you should consider asking yourself when you set a new goal is, "What will be possible in my life when I achieve this goal that isn't possible now?" We have the power to choose how we want to grow through the goals that we set for ourselves. One person may choose to climb Mount Everest to challenge themselves and discover who they are, whereas another person may start their own business. The journey is the reward. If a helicopter dropped the person who wants to climb Mount Everest at the peak, though they reached their desired outcome, nothing about them would change internal because they bypassed the input phase of the journey where the most learning occurs.

What we're willing to do to get what we want says more about who we are than what we want does. How we get what we want speaks volumes. Each of us is at point A on our own journey and we're trying to get to point B. Goals require us to step outside of our comfort zone. It is impossible to reach new heights without changing your who you are. People who play the lottery believe in luck over effort and are trying to change what they have and where they are in life without changing who they are first. The odds are against them.

There are thousands of ways to accomplish almost any goal. Two people can want money, but whereas one person is willing to steal to get it, the other person may not be. You can lie, steal, or cheat to get to where you want to go, but you would essentially be robbing yourself of the opportunity to see what you're really made of by trying to cut corners. We learn who we are in the authentic pursuit of becoming who we want to be. **To accomplish a goal and lose one's self in the process is worse than not accomplishing it and keeping one's sense of self. At the end of the day, it doesn't really matter what you're after—who you become in pursuit of your goals is what's most important.**

If you can't enjoy the journey, then you shouldn't go along for the ride. In most cases, the moment of achievement is only a fraction of the time it takes to get to that moment. With that in mind, you can learn to experience more fulfillment in pursuit of your goals if you focus on the enjoyment of giving your entire self to something you want, knowing that the declaration and dedication to that goal will lead to outcomes beyond your wildest imagination.

According to Edwin Locke, an American psychologist and pioneer in goal setting theory, goals have two characteristics: the goal's content and the goal's intensity.

The content refers to the outcome that we expect or what we actually want to achieve. The intensity refers to the amount of input or physical and mental resources needed to create and achieve the outcome. Locke's theory suggests that the best outcomes occur when:

» Goals required more input or were harder to achieve— not easier
» Goals had specific outcomes—especially quantitative
» Goals offered feedback or measurement during the input process
» The goal setter felt committed and ownership of the goal
» The goal setter's self-efficacy was high enough to believe that it was attainable

If harder goals yield better outcomes than easier goals, Locke's research implies that in addition to setting goals for particular outcomes, we should also set goals to challenge ourselves. Goal setting is not all about getting something out at the end—instead they are about seeing how much we are willing to put in to accomplish something we want. Locke's theory also speaks to feedback, suggesting that we want to know how we are improving along the way. Your growth along the journey is equally as important as the outcome. The outcome is just a manifestation of your growth. Your growth is what positions you to accomplish the next big thing.

Ultimately, we set goals because we value the experience of moving from Point A to Point B physically, mentally, spiritually, financially, and professionally. If that was not true, we would simply stop once we achieved a particular goal, but instead of stopping we set new goals that require more input from us, thus pushing us to the our highest potential. We could gain so much from the goal achievement process if we created goals that caused us to act in good ways that we haven't before and are more aligned with who we ultimately want to be.

In essence, many of us are afraid of heights—our highest selves. The reality is that many of us don't know the heights we're able to reach because we have never truly tried to push ourselves to our highest heights. It's one thing to climb to the peak of Mount Everest, but it's another thing to reach your personal peak. Many people settle for good enough when they have the potential be great.

There was a young basketball player that could jump really high. His coach wanted to test his leaping ability so he asked the young man to take out his chewing gum and stick it as high as he could on the backboard. So the young man does it and sticks the gum three quarters up the backboard, which is over 11.5 feet high. The coach asked him if that was his highest and he responded "Yes." He asked again and the player said "Yes."

So the coach grabbed a nearby ladder and climbed up to the backboard. He reached into his pocket and took out a roll of tape and a $100 bill from his wallet and taped it so that the bottom of the $100 bill was 3 inches higher than the gum. As he climbed down the ladder, he challenged the young man by saying that if he could grab the $100 off of the backboard he could keep it. The young man accepted the challenge, ran, jumped, and grabbed the $100 bill. Of course, the lesson was that his original jump that he claimed was his highest wasn't actually his highest, but with a little push, he could go higher.

I've discovered that it's not until you push something to its limits that you realize that it's limitless. Alicia Keys captured this best in one her lyrics that reads "And the day came when the risk it took to remain tightly closed in a bud was more painful than the risk it took to bloom." Guaranteed Goals gives you a coach in the form of your friends, an incentive in the form of your *why*, and a challenge to be great in the form of your goal. In order to achieve better outcomes *and* income (spiritually, financially, socially, etc) in your lives, you have to be willing to put more into yourself.

DEALING WITH FAILURE

If you don't succeed, that's okay. Not succeeding doesn't equal failure. Failure only comes from not trying. **When we fail, we usually fail forward and thus are further along than we would have been if we didn't try.** Oftentimes when someone doesn't succeed at their 30 Day Do It, it is because they either overestimated what they were capable of at the moment or their strategy was wrong despite their effort. If you overestimated yourself, now you have a more accurate assessment of who you are and what you're willing to do to get what you want and where you want. **If you gave 100% effort, but your strategy was wrong, don't get down on yourself. Instead, give 100% effort to a new strategy. It's not always about trying harder—sometimes we just have to be smarter about how we try.**

What is failure anyway? Is it the end or the beginning? Why are we so afraid of it? How can we change our relationship to it? According to the dictionary, failure means:
1. lack of success: a lack of success in or at something.
2. something less than that required: something that falls short of what is required or expected.
3. somebody or something that fails: somebody or something that is unsuccessful.

I define failure as the moment we stop investing in something we believe in because of overwhelming and unwelcomed feedback.

We tend to think of failure as the end result of something, but there is actually a moment after a product, project, or person thinks they are finished when they decide that the feedback overwhelms their faith. Therefore, instead of iterating on the seemingly end result, we decide to stop investing entirely in something that only needs minor tweaks.

Perfectionism definitely leads to more failures than anything else. With perfectionist, the feedback is often internal and in their own mind, and their goal or project never makes it into the world at all because they're seeking an unreal state. **Perfection can't be reached without feedback.** Most products, projects, and goals fail before anyone else even knows about their existence.

For those that do enter the world, sometimes the feedback is so tough (i.e. things aren't going the way you want, users aren't coming in droves, it's not selling, etc.) that they give up. On any project timeline, the "shipping" of the product to market is only the halfway mark if that. The hardest work comes after the idea and reality meet. The project fails when the person stops at this point.

It's not failure that we fear. It's fear of going backwards, being behind, losing ground. Ironically, failure rarely leads to any of those. In my life, there have been times where I perceived something as a failure, but someone else saw it in another way and helped me discover how to repurpose it and make it more valuable. (Perceived) failure has only propelled me forward because of how I've been able to listen when something doesn't go as expected. But if we close ourselves off at the moment rich feedback is ready to be given, we miss the opportunity to learn.

Failure is never a dead end. It's a time for pruning, correction, and redirection. It's a necessary coach to help you decide how bad you want success. If success came easy, then we would undervalue it—success would become average and then there would be something else we pursue to prove our skills. If we follow failure for long enough in our authentic attempt to achieve success, it will eventually lead us to success. If we adopt an identity as a failure, meaning that failure is our destiny, that's what where we'll end up. **People aren't failures—our processes fail.**

I wrote a letter called Dear Failure, that may be helpful for you to read and write for yourself. It changed my relationship to this ephemeral thing we call failure. When we focus on our input more than the outcome, failure becomes less relevant and we can simply see it as feedback for our next step.

Dear Failure

Dear Failure,

I remember when we first met. You were wearing all black and I was afraid of you. At the time, I was dating Good Enough. I didn't want to take a risk on you. With Good Enough, I was safe, secure, and comfortable. But Good Enough wasn't good enough. I needed more. I needed to be pushed...be challenged.

That's when we met face-to-face. I guess opposites attract. Who would have thought that a Successful and a Failure would date. It's like mixing vinegar and oil or a

---

Capulet and a Montague. I acted like I couldn't stand you, but when I relaxed and just truly embraced you, I learned so much from you. I wish more people got to know you like me and would stop judging you.

You remember who introduced us? My first business introduced us back in 2005. All my other friends hated you. But I didn't care what they said. I had to see for myself what you were all about. I invested my time, money, energy, and identity in you. You showed me things about myself that I didn't even know about like my ego and my self-doubt. You knew how to press my buttons and now I know myself better.

I know I ran away when we broke up. It was me, not you. In hindsight, I have to admit that you made me better. And for that I want to say thank you.

I have a feeling that I'll be seeing you around. I hear you're out there still breaking hearts. I don't want the next time we meet to be awkward.

As you'd always say, "If you fall out of love with a Failure, make sure you fail forward."

Sincerely,

Mr. Successful

Good Execution of this Principle

"It's too hard."

You want to become a better public speaker because you're certain that it will help you get promoted at work. So you sign up for Toastmasters and start going to classes once a month. You forgot about your fear of public speaking. It's so easy to watch others speak. In your first speech you stutter, say "um", and get dry mouth. Your speech ends with "It's too hard," and you're ready to give up. After being encouraged by one of the leaders, you realize that this is less about the promotion and more about your personal growth and development. Every few weeks, you get an opportunity to learn about new topics that others address and you get to delve into your various interests as you prepare for your speeches. In addition, you establish new friendships and develop confidence that transcends the workplace. After a few months, you decided to compete regionally. Your speech in the regional competition is titled "The Journey Is The Reward." You have successfully overcome your fear of public speaking and achieved a more perfect picture of who you really are.

APPLICATION:
Plan, Perform, & Perfect

CASE STUDY: LEBRON JAMES

HOW LEBRON JAMES GUARANTEED HIS FIRST NBA CHAMPIONSHIP

I'm a huge Lebron James fan. I study his game and replay his post-game comments to understand his thinking. I am inspired by his journey to greatness and tireless work ethic. Like Lebron, I believe we all have a unique talent, but that doesn't guarantee our greatness. The difference is how we shape that talent through our goals.

For Lebron James, New Year's Day is not January 1st. It's the last day of the NBA season. After losing to the Dallas Mavericks in Game 7 of the 2011 NBA Finals, he went into a dark place—a place where I believe he dug deep and set goals for the upcoming season using these 9 questions, which ultimately resulted in an MVP, his first NBA Championship, and Finals MVP.

Like Lebron, every year in early January, many people set New Year's resolutions. Within 30 days, their aspirational piece of paper is buried under a pile of day-to-day life. After many failed attempts, most people would say that "New Year's resolutions don't work."

CASE STUDY: LEBRON JAMES

1. EXPERIENCE: I ultimately want to experience what it is like to be…

We don't set goals for the sake of setting goals. When we do that, our goals just become another to-do list item and that's not inspiring. The main reason we set goals is because we want to have a new experience in or of life. As we examine our current life, we see an opportunity to change, grow, and improve our lives in such a way that our experience of it is even better than before.

When someone sets a goal to lose weight, they are really saying that they want to experience what it is like to be healthy, full of energy, and alive. When someone sets a goal to change jobs, they don't just want a new title and company. They are really saying that they want to experience what it is like to live in their strengths daily, make a visible impact, and be rewarded fairly for the results they create.

When we start with the experience we want to create first, it opens us up to a variety of different goals we can set to gain that experience. For instance, if I want to experience financial freedom, there are lots of different goals or approaches that may get me there such as paying off my credit card debt, starting my side hustle after work, buying an income property, learning how to day-trade, reducing my cost of living, or increasing my income.

Before we start doing anything, it's important to determine who we have to be to do it. That's the greatest and hardest change to make of all—a change in your being. If I want to lose weight, but I'm lazy, then doing P90x isn't going to work for me, but perhaps there is a diet that will. If I want financial freedom, but my being loves to splurge on clothes, food, and travel, then reducing my expenses won't work for me—instead

CASE STUDY: LEBRON JAMES

I have to figure out how to make more income. By starting with the experience, you can choose the goal that is best for who you are, and who you ultimately want to be as well as where you are in relationship to your desired destination.

Lebron James' Application:

At the end of the 2011 NBA season, Lebron James was experiencing what it was like to be a great NBA player who led two different teams to the NBA finals, but lost twice. He was not happy with that experience. He didn't just want to be a great player. He wanted to experience what it was like to be an NBA champion multiple times.

CASE STUDY: LEBRON JAMES

2. INTENTION: Why is having this experience so important to me beyond just doing it?

The moment we declare what we want to be and experience, our tendency is to jump straight into doing and action. But before we do anything, it is important to establish our "why". Why is having this experience so important to us? Victor Frankl once said, "A man who knows his why can bear almost any how." Sometimes it's not that we don't know how to do something. Sometimes our why isn't big enough and our inaction shows us that.

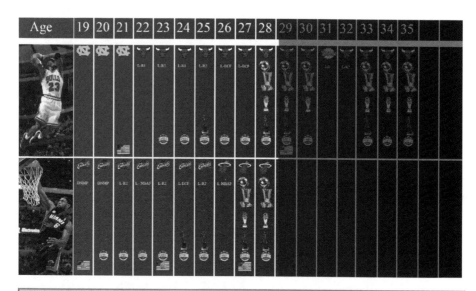

Age	19	20	21	22	23	24	25	26	27	28	29	30	31	32	33	34	35		

Lebron James' Application:

Lebron James has said this in several interviews. He has one goal. He wants to be the greatest basketball player of all-time. Period. That's his why. He doesn't want to be the Dan Marino of the NBA. Great players win championships—plural.

CASE STUDY: LEBRON JAMES

3. GROWTH: What limiting beliefs or fears will be pushed by this experience?

Goals should require you to grow into someone you haven't been before. An activity that doesn't require growth is merely a to do list item. If you accomplished all of your goals last year, you likely underestimated your abilities and didn't challenge yourself. If you didn't accomplish them all, you may have overestimated your abilities. This is where a "30 Day Do It" can provide great opportunities. They challenge the chatter in our heads "That I can't...", "That I'm too...", "That people won't...."

A great example of a 30 Day Do It would be running a marathon in a certain time when you've only run half-marathons up until this point. Another example would be achieving sales of $20,000 in a week, when your personal best is currently at $15,000. A 30 Day Do It should stretch you in a way that creates some uncertainty, but also inspires you. This should challenge your limiting beliefs and expand your self-concept.

Lebron James' Application:

Lebron James' #1 limiting belief was "That I have to do it on my own." He tried to carry the Cleveland Cavaliers on his back to a championship. In the first 7 years of his career, he took a team whose record the season before he was drafted was 17-65 to 61-21 in his last year with them. But by the time he got to the NBA Finals or the Eastern Conference Finals, he was beat and you could see it in his demeanor and stamina in both elimination games. He didn't give up, but his tank was empty.

CASE STUDY: LEBRON JAMES

4. GAPS: What challenges or excuses do I see/foresee stopping me from creating this experience?

Before we even set new goals, many of us have our excuses ready in the back of our minds. Instead of dealing with our excuses after trying to achieve our goals, why not just deal with them all upfront. Let's say "Excuse me excuses. I'm going to get you out the way now because having this experience is important to me and nothing is going to stop me."

Imagine yourself 30 days into the future. Imagine that you failed miserably at the goal you set. What would be all of the reason you didn't do what you said you wanted to do? We know all of the commons ones—I don't have time. The kids. I didn't have the money. I was too tired. Work got busy. My boss this and that. My wife this and that. I didn't have any support. One of my favorite quotes is "Excuses are monuments of nothingness. They build bridges to nowhere. Those who use these tools of incompetence, seldom become anything but nothing at all."

CASE STUDY: LEBRON JAMES

Lebron James' Application:

As stated before, Lebron James knew that at the end of his career, if he didn't win an NBA championship, that his top two excuses would be that he didn't have role players around him and that he never had a great coach. When you think about who was on Michael Jordan's and Kobe Bryant's NBA championship teams, immediately names like Scottie Pippen, Dennis Rodman, Steve Kerr, Shaq, and Pau Gasol come to mind. If I ask you who was on Lebron's Cleveland team that made it to the 2007 NBA Finals, who comes to mind? Nobody…unless you live in Cleveland. On top of that, Michael Jordan and Kobe Bryant had Phil Jackson, the greatest coach in NBA history. So these were two gaps that Lebron could try to fill (no pun intended) in advance.

CASE STUDY: LEBRON JAMES

5. SUPPORT: How can I attempt to close these gaps in advance? Who/what can help me successfully create this experience?

Anytime we feel stuck or reach a plateau in our life, it's usually because we have exhausted our know-how. In those moments, we end up doing more of the same. We hustle harder instead of hustling smarter.

When you don't know how to breakthrough to a new level, one of the easiest things you can do is look for a course, on coaching, or consulting. A course will give you new information and insights. This will allow you to look at your situation with a new lens. Coaching will give you accountability and another perspective. Perhaps you have a blind spot or you're procrastinating on doing that very thing which makes the difference you seek. And a consultant will do what they can to get you to who and where you want to be with as little energy and effort as possible from you.these tools of incompetence, seldom become anything but nothing at all."

CASE STUDY: LEBRON JAMES

Lebron James' Application:

In 2010, Lebron made "The Decision" to join Dwayne Wade and Chris Bosh in Miami, where he would have support. Both players were already All-Stars. And Dwayne Wade (along with Shaq) carried the Miami Heat to their first NBA championship, which was the experience Lebron James was trying to have.

The stars would have had to align perfectly for Lebron James to get Phil Jackson as his coach. Pat Riley was even an option for a moment. But there is only so much you can control and he got the young Erik Spoelstra instead. Obviously the most important thing was that he finally got his supporting cast.

CASE STUDY: LEBRON JAMES

6. EFFORT: What are the actions that I am 100% accountable for to create this experience?

When you set a goal, differentiate between the action and the outcome. You can only hold yourself 100% accountable to the action and the effort required to complete the action. You may do the action with all of your effort and still not achieve your desired outcome. For instance, you can go to the gym every day for 3 months and still not lose the 20 pounds you desired if your workout plan wasn't right.

This is where a coach, friend, mentor, professional, or colleague comes in—they help improve your strategy. They can help you make sure that you are engaged in right action through feedback, while you focus on right effort. The world and the economy are evolving faster than ever and sometimes what we want and desire doesn't come to us in the exact way or form we expected it to. So be open—meaning hold onto your plan loosely, but stand firm in your intention.

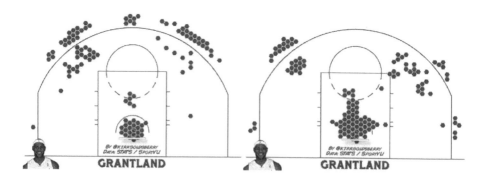

MOST COMMON SHOT LOCATIONS

LAST YEAR IN CLEVELAND, 2009-2010   FIRST YEAR IN MIAMI, 2010-2011

CASE STUDY: LEBRON JAMES

Lebron James' Application:

In his last year in Cleveland, Lebron played and shot more like a point guard. He had tons of 3-point attempts. In his first year in Miami, he had a lot less. And in his second year in Miami, most of his points were in the paint. He earned easier baskets because he made an intentional choice to work on his low-post game. He also altered his off-season and in-season physical training program so that he could endure the playoffs, not just the regular season. These were things that were 100% in his control regarding how he spent his time.

CASE STUDY: LEBRON JAMES

7. INITIATION: What is the "first domino?" What's the easiest action I can do right now that will set my experience in motion?

Dates don't hold you accountable—events that involve other people and deliverables do. If you're serious about accomplishing a goal, create an event that involves other people where you will share a deliverable. A deliverable can be a document you create, photos, a proposal, or a demonstration (i.e. you weighing yourself in front of your accountability partners). It serves as proof that you did what you said you were going to do.

I wrote this book in 30 days by sending an email to 100 friends and telling them that I would send them the first draft in 30 days. By doing that, I activated positive peer pressure and I delivered. As human beings, we have a weird psychology about us where we are more comfortable disappointing ourselves than we are other people. So use it to your advantage by getting other people involved and promising to show them the results of your effort. For you, it may mean sending invitations, paying a coach or trainer, buying your tickets, or giving a friend $100 if I don't do what you say. Do whatever works for you.

CASE STUDY: LEBRON JAMES

Lebron James' Application:

Lebron's first domino was to schedule low-post training in the off-season with Hakeem Olajuwon, one of the best low-post players of all-time. Once those sessions were schedule, Lebron just had to show up and Hakeem would guide him through the rest. He invested in coaching and used his coaching as a source of accountability to become the player and champion he said he wanted to be.

CASE STUDY: LEBRON JAMES

8. MEASUREMENT: How will I measure my success during the experience?

Focus on your input and the journey as much as the outcome and the destination. Your life is your vehicles to design, drive, and maintain. Thus, you need a dashboard. Though a dashboard has no functional use in a car getting from point A to point B, it lets you know how well the vehicle is doing along the way by measuring how hard, how hot, how far, and how full the car is. Without a dashboard, you could overheat, run out of gas, or break the speed limit.

I invite you all to create a visual dashboard for yourselves. Rather than leaving your goals as words, make a one-pager that has bar graphs, pie charts, or check boxes so that you can visually see where you are along your journey this year. If you have a savings goal of of $20,000, put a big bar graph on the back of your bedroom door and color it in as your savings grow. If you're giving up smoking, pin a $10 bill to a calendar for each day you don't smoke to symbolize what you would have spent on a pack and celebrate that you didn't. Make it visual. Other examples of measurements include pounds lost, running time, dollars earned, and # of new clients.

2007 Cleveland Cavaliers

G	GS	MP	FG	FGA	FG%	3P	3PA	3P%	FT	FTA	FT%	ORB	DRB	TRB	AST	STL	BLK	TOV	PF	PTS	GmSc	Player
6	6	46.2	8.8	19.7	0.449	0.8	2.3	0.357	7.2	9.7	0.741	1.2	8.0	9.2	8.5	2.7	0.5	3.2	1.3	25.7	22.9	James
6	6	32.3	5.2	10.3	0.5	0.0	0.0		2.5	3.2	0.789	3.0	6.0	9.0	1.0	0.5	0.8	1.3	2.7	12.8	10.7	Ilgauskas
6	0	24.9	3.0	6.5	0.462	2.0	4.0	0.5	5.5	6.2	0.892	1.0	1.8	2.8	1.3	0.5	0.5	1.2	3.2	13.5	10.5	Gibson
6	0	25.6	3.0	6.5	0.462	0.0	0.3	0	1.5	2.8	0.529	3.0	3.3	6.3	0.3	1.3	0.7	1.3	3.5	7.5	6.0	Varejao
6	6	26.6	4.0	9.0	0.444	0.0	0.0		1.2	1.7	0.7	1.5	3.5	5.0	0.7	0.8	0.2	1.7	3.2	9.2	4.9	Gooden
6	6	33.8	3.7	9.3	0.393	1.0	2.7	0.375	0.8	1.7	0.5	0.5	2.3	2.8	1.5	1.0	0.0	1.3	2.8	9.2	4.4	Pavlovic
6	6	29.8	2.3	6.8	0.341	0.7	1.5	0.444	1.8	2.7	0.688	0.3	2.5	2.8	2.2	1.2	0.2	2.0	1.8	7.2	4.0	Hughes
6	0	13.5	1.2	3.7	0.318	0.7	2.3	0.286	0.0	0.0		0.5	1.8	2.3	0.0	0.0	0.5	0.2	2.2	3.0	1.1	Marshall
5	0	6.6	0.0	1.0	0	0.0	0.2	0	0.4	0.8	0.5	0.2	0.4	0.6	0.6	0.6	0.0	0.2	0.2	0.4	0.5	Snow
5	0	12.3	0.6	2.8	0.214	0.4	2.4	0.167	0.0	0.0		0.0	0.6	0.6	1.0	0.0	0.0	0.0	1.4	1.6	0.2	Jones

CASE STUDY: LEBRON JAMES

2013 Miami Heat

G	GS	MP	FG	FGA	FG%	3P	3PA	3P%	FT	FTA	FT%	ORB	DRB	TRB	AST	STL	BLK	TOV	PF	PTS	GmSc	Player
6	6	43.9	10.8	21.0	0.516	2.3	5.3	0.438	4.5	6.3	0.711	1.8	5.3	7.2	5.5	1.3	1.5	3.0	2.8	28.5	22.4	James
6	6	38.1	5.7	12.8	0.442	0.2	0.5	0.333	3.0	4.5	0.667	1.7	2.8	4.5	4.8	1.3	1.2	2.5	2.8	14.5	11.1	Wade
6	6	26.9	4.0	8.8	0.453	1.0	2.2	0.462	3.0	3.2	0.947	0.7	0.8	1.5	3.0	1.0	0.0	1.2	3.5	12.0	8.6	Chalmers
5	0	18.4	3.0	3.0	1	0.0	0.0		1.2	1.4	0.857	1.6	3.0	4.6	0.0	0.4	1.6	0.2	3.2	7.2	8.3	Anderson
6	6	31.8	3.8	9.3	0.411	1.2	2.3	0.5	2.5	3.0	0.833	0.5	3.2	3.7	0.7	0.5	0.7	1.0	3.0	11.3	6.7	Bosh
6	6	19.5	3.3	5.3	0.625	0.0	0.0		0.3	0.5	0.667	1.5	2.5	4.0	0.5	0.8	0.2	0.8	2.8	7.0	5.7	Haslem
6	0	19.6	1.8	4.7	0.393	0.5	1.5	0.333	0.3	0.3	1	0.3	1.3	1.7	1.7	0.5	0.2	1.0	1.5	4.5	2.8	Cole
6	0	22.8	2.2	7.7	0.283	1.2	4.0	0.292	1.2	1.8	0.636	0.7	2.5	3.2	0.7	0.7	0.2	1.0	1.3	6.7	2.8	Allen
4	0	8.9	0.3	1.5	0.167	0.0	0.0		0.0	0.0		1.3	1.0	2.3	0.0	0.3	0.8	0.0	2.0	0.5	0.7	Anthony
6	0	16.1	0.3	2.7	0.125	0.3	2.5	0.133	1.3	1.7	0.8	0.5	1.0	1.5	0.2	0.2	0.3	0.3	2.2	2.3	0.4	Battier

Lebron James' Application:

Lebron's metrics of success are clear based on his stat sheet. He is focused on increasing his points in the paint and field goal percentage and decreasing his turnovers and personal fouls. Most people celebrate number of points scored, but that isn't Lebron's focus anymore. He is not going for the scoring title. He wants to be a facilitator like Magic Johnson, getting his whole team involved, but at the same time be able to score at will from the inside or outside when his team needs him to. Ultimately, he believes that being this kind of player will improve his chances of winning another NBA championship with the Miami Heat.

CASE STUDY: LEBRON JAMES

9. AUTHENTICITY: Do I accept this goal as an authentic intentional choice of my own?

Look within and answer "Yes!" or "No." While our goals may be influenced by things we've heard and seen, in order to be fully committed, we have to fully own the goal as our own. People close to you can make recommendations and give advice, but at the end of the day, you have to determine if this is the right goal for you. Before you begin, get a clear "Yes!" or "No," and then go. The x-factor to success is knowing your "why". The clearer you are on the reason you are doing anything before you even begin, the more likely it is that you will succeed.

Lebron James' Application:

Every NBA player isn't seeking to be the greatest player of all-time. In fact, only a few probably ever consider it. For some, getting to the NBA was enough. For others, starting is another. For some, becoming an NBA all-star is enough. For Lebron, nothing is enough unless he becomes the great NBA basketball player of all-time.

USING THE WORKSHEETS

Congratulations! Now you understand the Guaranteed Goals principles and process of Authenticity, Accountability, and Activation and you are ready to put them into action. Using the worksheets below, which you can download at WWW.GUARANTEEDGOALS.COM, you can start setting more 30 Day Do Its that get you to where you want to go and transform who you are in the process.

If you accepted my challenge in the introduction of the book, your first Guaranteed Goals Group should be coming up soon. If not, then now is a great time to activate it by sending out invitations. Since you're almost done reading the book, you don't need to wait 30 days for the event.

The principles and processes of Guaranteed Goals have been carefully integrated into the worksheets. The first worksheet is the Guaranteed Goal Setting Worksheet and second one is the Guaranteed Goal Evaluation Worksheet. The worksheets guide you through a step-by-step process to set your next Guaranteed Goal. The Guaranteed Goal Evaluation Worksheet should be completed by the goal setter before the next Guaranteed Goal group.

The Guaranteed Goal Setting Worksheet is for use at the end of each Guaranteed Goals Group. The purpose of this worksheet is to make sure that your 30 Day Do It program is aligned with your Guaranteed Goal, define success, clarify your **why**, and get approval.

You should keep your worksheets in a folder so that you can observe your successful and unsuccessful patterns over time. This will help you improve at goal achievement so that you know what you need to do and put in place to accomplish any goal you have.

THE GUARANTEED GOAL SETTING WORKSHEET

STEP 1: CHOOSE A GOAL & 30 DAY DO IT
A. Declare your Guaranteed Goal (your desired outcome).
Example 1: Lose 10 pounds this month.
Example 2: Write the first 3 chapters of my book.
B. Define the 30 Day Do It you will do to achieve your goal.
Example 1: Follow the P90X program and diet for 30 days.
Example 2: Write from 6:30am-7:30am 5 days per week.
C. Estimate the approximate amount of time and money you need to set aside to achieve your goal.

STEP 2: AUTHENTICATE YOUR GOAL
A. Complete the seven prompts as thoroughly and specifically as possible as possible.

STEP 3: ACTIVATE THE GOAL
A. Determine your cost if you don't complete the goal to tip the balance.
B. Describe how you will set the goal in motion by finding the first domino and burning the boats. You can set it in motion via phone calls, text messaging, or emailing out invitations. You can also get online right away and pay for accountability by buying a plane ticket, a course, equipment, or time with a personal trainer or coach who will hold you accountable.

STEP 4: CREATE ACCOUNTABILITY
A. Set a date, time and location for your next meeting and celebration. If your celebrate is a separate event, be strategic about who you decide to invite. Invite people who will push you, inform you, and hold you accountable. It is assumed that Guaranteed Goals Group members will naturally support you in these ways.
B. Define how you will demonstrate your success.
C. Give your word by signing and dating the page.

1. CHOOSE A GOAL & 30 DAY DO IT

My Guaranteed Goal is to: _____

My 30 Day Do It is to: _____

In the next 30 days, I need to invest _____ hours and $_____ into the completion of my 30 Day Do It.

GUARANTEED GOALS

2. AUTHENTICATE YOUR GOAL

CLARIFY WHY THIS & WHY NOW

1. I ultimately want to **experience** what it's like to be:

2. My **intention** and reason why this is so important is that:

3. I will **grow** by challenging my limiting beliefs & fears such as:

4. **Gaps** I foresee potentially derailing my goal include:

5. To close those gaps in advance I need **support** from/on:

6. The actions I will give 100% **effort** to & am 100% in control of include:

7. I will **measure** my success along the way in the form of:

3. ACTIVATE THE GOAL

TIP THE BALANCE

If I don't complete my 30 Day Do It, I commit to:

I will find the first domino & burn the boat by:

4. CREATE ACCOUNTABILITY

PLAN TO CELEBRATE

My celebration and next meeting is on: ___/____ at_____pm

Location:_____

PLAN TO DEMONSTRATE

I will show proof of my success to the group by:_____

GIVE YOUR WORD

I will do whatever it takes to uphold my word.

My signature:

Date: _____/____

---

1. CHOOSE A GOAL & 30 DAY DO IT

My Guaranteed Goal is to: *Make it easier for 30 Day Do It Groups to self-organize*

My 30 Day Do It is to: *Create an online system that allows people organize easily*

In the next 30 days, I need to invest *20* hours and $*500* into the completion of my 30 Day Do It.

GUARANTEED GOALS

2. AUTHENTICATE YOUR GOAL

CLARIFY WHY THIS & WHY NOW

1. I ultimately want to **experience** what it's like to be:
a person who impacts people's lives globally

2. My **intention** and reason why this is so important is that:
Serving people 1-on-1 or through speaking can be limiting and I want to reach people all over the world

3. I will **grow** by challenging my limiting beliefs & fears such as:
I have to be physically present for change to occur

4. **Gaps** I foresee potentially derailing my goal include:
Current and Prospective 30 Day Do It members

5. To close those gaps in advance I need **support** from/on:
Keith (my web developer) and at least Living Room Leaders to test out the system & give feedback

6. The actions I will give 100% **effort** to & am 100% in control of include: *Creating the designs, Reaching to Living Room Leaders, Compiling feedback, Supporting Keith*

7. I will **measure** my success along the way in the form of:
# of bugs, quantity and quality of feedback

3. ACTIVATE THE GOAL

TIP THE BALANCE

If I don't complete my 30 Day Do It, I commit to:
Giving each of my group members $50

I will find the first domino & burn the boat by:
Paying the web developer 50% up front tomorrow

4. CREATE ACCOUNTABILITY

PLAN TO CELEBRATE

My celebration and next meeting is on: *2/28* at *6* pm

Location: *Jennifer's at 1000 Successful Way*

PLAN TO DEMONSTRATE

I will show proof of my success to the group by: *Showing my group the technology "as is" at the meeting*

GIVE YOUR WORD

I will do whatever it takes to uphold my word.

My signature: *Jullien Gordon*

Date: *2/1*

PRINT THIS WORKSHEET FOR FREE AT
WWW.GUARANTEEDGOALS.COM

129

THE GUARANTEED GOAL EVALUATION WORKSHEET

STEP 5: DID YOU SUCCEED?

A. Define your results. Mark yes, no, or sort of—in unexpected ways.

STEP 6: SUCCESSFUL & UNSUCCESSFUL PATTERNS

A. Evaluate your successful patterns so that you can learn about yourself and your process. If you achieved your goal, answer all of the questions in column one and only the ones that apply in column two.
B. Evaluate your unsuccessful patterns. If you didn't achieve your goal, answer all of the questions in column two. If you sort of achieve your goal, answer all of the questions that apply.

STEP 7: CELEBRATION

If you achieved your goal:
A. Verify that your celebration occurred by getting someone there to sign this page.
B. Sign and date this page when your celebrate your achievement.

If you did not achieve your goal:
A. Verify that your payment occurred by getting someone there to sign this page.
B. Sign and date this page when you complete your payment from step 3 on the first page.

5. DID I SUCCEED?

[ ] YES [ ] NO [ ] SORT OF—IN UNEXPECTED WAYS

6. SUCCESSFUL & UNSUCCESSFUL HABITS

In achieving my 30 Day Do It, I learned that I: _____

_____

One thing I would do differently next time is: _____

_____

I was motivated most by: _____

_____

Supportive people included: _____

_____

What worked for me: _____

_____

Unexpected outcomes included: _____

_____

My bad excuses included: _____

_____

Next time, I can prevent these excuses by: _____

_____

I was demotivated most by: _____

_____

Unsupportive people included: _____

_____

What didn't work for me: _____

_____

Unexpected obstacles included: _____

_____

7. CELEBRATION OR PAYMENT

PROOF OF CELEBRATION

Signature of a group member:

_____

My Signature:

_____

Date: ____/____

PROOF OF PAYMENT

Signature of a group member:

_____

My Signature:

_____

Date: ____/____

---

5. DID I SUCCEED?

[X] YES [ ] NO [ ] SORT OF—IN UNEXPECTED WAYS

6. SUCCESSFUL & UNSUCCESSFUL HABITS

In achieving my 30 Day Do It, I learned that I: *Need to start right away to build momentum*

One thing I would do differently next time is: *Call people I need to help in the first 3 days*

I was motivated most by: *The vision of an international movement and the $500 I would have to pay*

Supportive people included: *Pam Jackson, Keith Smith & Stephen Moore, Leslie Schnyder, Jimmie Jays*

What worked for me: *Creating a detailed to do list & setting aside 2 hours every day to execute*

Unexpected outcomes included: *People started using the database and found it extremely useful*

My bad excuses included: *Not knowing if this was the the most valuable way to be spending my time*

Next time, I can prevent these excuses by: *Interview a few goal setters first to see what they really want*

I was demotivated most by: *Other personal issues that came up during the month*

Unsupportive people included: *None*

What didn't work for me: *Having to rely on other people who I know are extremely busy already*

Unexpected obstacles included: *Having to learn a new technology in only a few weeks*

7. CELEBRATION OR PAYMENT

PROOF OF CELEBRATION

Signature of a group member:

Toni Daniles

My Signature:

Jullien Gordon

Date: *2/28*

PROOF OF PAYMENT

Signature of a group member:

_____

My Signature:

_____

Date: ____/____

PRINT THIS WORKSHEET FOR FREE AT
WWW.GUARANTEEDGOALS.COM

AFTERWORD

This is the end of the New Year's resolution and the birth of the New Month's Resolution. Too many people read personal development books only to procrastinate from doing the real work necessary to transform their lives. One of my core principles is that personal development isn't always personal. In fact, collective accountability and teams are the key ingredients to accomplishing your goals. I want to see positive transformation in your life and the lives of those around you and Guaranteed Goals Groups are one way accomplish that.

I've been successfully using the Guaranteed Goal Setting process in my own life, with my students, and with my coaching clients. This book is evidence that it works! It's time to stop waiting on the world to move for you and start moving your world forward. I realized that if I'm going to change the world, I need a world of change in me and Guaranteed Goals is how I'm creating that change for myself and for others.

My purpose is to help as many people as possible find and align their lives with their purpose. Purpose is the ultimate goal. Purpose is a way of living rather than a particular end result or destination. In my first book *The 8 Cylinders of Success*, I outlined 8 ways to explore your purpose. But even after someone finds their purpose, the true challenge is committing to align their life with it through action. I believe that our purpose is the one thing that is guaranteed to bring us success, but fear and lack of motivation cause us to still make excuses. *The 8 Cylinders of Success* is all about where to go in life and *Guaranteed Goals* is all about how to get there.

I integrate Guaranteed Goals into all of my work and relationships to push myself and those around me to their highest selves. One of my greatest success stories came from a student in one of my Driving School for Life courses. At the end of the course, each student is required to set a 30 Day Do It in order to put the rubber to the road. This student wanted to transition from what she was doing to becoming a full-time life coach so she decided to host a vision boarding party at her home to attract potential clients. Seventeen days after her course, she sent me the message below via Facebook.

As a result of taking her 30 Day Do It seriously, she earned an additional $1200 over the next 3 months off of a few hundred dollar investment in herself via the Driving School for Life Course. There aren't any stocks in the market yielding that kind of return.

But what's even more powerful about the story above is that her two clients came before she even completed her 30 Day Do It. By simply having the invitations to the vision boarding party ready to talk about, she was able to attract and convince new life coaching clients that she was the one for them. **Oftentimes, we look for the reward at the end of the goal, but in most cases, the rewards lie along the journey.**

Your authentic pursuit of your Guaranteed Goals each month can lead to amazing possibilities beyond the accomplishment of the goal itself. **At the end of the day, it's not the goal we really want—it's the new lifestyle that is achieved through accomplishing the goal.** Bruce Lee once said "A *goal* is not always meant to be reached, it often serves simply as something to *aim* at." For my client, the lifestyle she wanted is one of a life coach and people started

JULLIEN!!! OMG!

I just wanted to let you know that I had a huge breakthrough regarding life coaching. I actually got a paying client who offered me 5 times what I requested AND committed to 3 months. I also have another who is interested in talking to me about coaching. This has all come out of talking to people about having that party at my house to create vision boards.

I walked into your class knowing I wanted to be a life coach but afraid to charge for something I would normally do for free. That fear stopped me from even trying to create what I wanted most in life. After doing DSFL, I took your 30 day challenge seriously which opened up a series of conversations and lead to PAYING CLIENTS, my own business and feeling more fulfilled as a human being than I have ever felt before.

While I still have a day job, I am confident that this is only the very beginning and I marvel when I think of how much more there is to come. I would like to be doing this full time by next year and now I know I can! Thanks for standing for who people are at their essence. Keep being who you are being.

GOD BLESS!

seeing her as a life coach before her first vision boarding party or certification because of her 30 Day Do It.

My next big goal is to create the world's largest and most effective purpose-driven goal setting movement ever and I invite you to join me. Imagine thousands of people in their living rooms worldwide setting Guaranteed Goals together. I believe in building community through goal setting. There are communities for public speaking, overcoming alcoholism, and reading books, but there aren't many communities that I know of for pure goal setting. Together, we can to put an end to the New Year's resolution and introduce the New Month's resolution and Guaranteed Goal Setting.

I wish you best on your journey, your goals, and first Guaranteed Goals Group. Thank you for your commitment to yourself and the self-development of those around you.

Godspeed!

MY MONTHLY DASHBOARD

....
Goal Achiever's Name   Guaranteed Goals Group's Name

Due												
My Score	1	2	3	4	5	6	7	8	9	10	11	12
Group Score	1	2	3	4	5	6	7	8	9	10	11	12

LEGEND: successful = +1, sort of = +0.5, new goal setter = +0.5, unsuccessful = 0, absent = -1

\# New Goal Setters   \# Hosted

☐ ☐ ☐ ☐ ☐ ☐ ☐ ☐ ☐   ☐ ☐ ☐

What did I accomplish this month?

JANUARY..

FEBRUARY..

MARCH...

APRIL...

MAY...

JUNE..

JULY..

AUGUST...

SEPTEMBER...

OCTOBER...

NOVEMBER...

DECEMBER...

30 DAY DO IT PROGRAMS

Find Your Purpose
Personal Branding
Lose 10 Pounds
Write A Book
Love Yourself
Career Transition
Quit Smoking
Make More Money
Start A Business
Find Your Passion
Get Organized
Find More Friends
Grad School: Find A Program
Grad School: Get In A Program
Get Promoted
The Perfect Partner
Conversation With God
Embody A Characteristic
Break The Habit
Amazing Mentor
Create Something
Learn A Language
Become An Expert
Write A Business Plan
Say No & Let Go

WWW.GUARANTEEDGOALS.COM

BIBLIOGRAPHY

"Divorce Rate In America." Online. Copyright 2009.
September 27, 2009.
http://www.divorcerate.org

Myers, Paul. Need to Know. TalkBiz News, 2009.

Zock, Hetty. A Psychology of Ultimate Concern (Psychology
of Religion). Rodopi, 1990.

Frankl, Victor. Man's Search for Meaning. Boston,
Massachusetts: Beacon Press, 2006.

Reiss, Steven. Who am I? The 16 Basic Desires that
Motivate Our Actions and Define Our Personalities. New
York, NY: Berkley Trade, 2002.

"Top Ten New Year's Resolutions." Online. Copyright.
September 27, 2009.
http://www.goalsguy.com/events/n_top-ten-resolutions.html

Damon, William. The Path To Purpose: How Young People
Find Their Calling in Life. New York, NY: Free Press, 2009.

Gordon, Jullien. The 8 Cylinders of Success: How To Align
Your Personal & Professional Purpose. New York, NY:
Department of Motivated Vehicles, 2009.

Norcross JC, Mrykalo MS, Blagys MD. (2002). Auld Lang
Syne: Success predictors, change processes, and self-
reported outcomes of New Year's resolvers and
nonresolvers. *Journal of Clinical Psychology,* 58:397-405

Balci R, Aghazadeh F. (2003). The effect of work-rest schedules and type of task on the discomfort and performance of VDT users. *Ergonomics*, 15;46(5):455-65.

"Parkinson's Law." Online. Copyright 2009. September 27, 2009.
http://en.wikipedia.org/wiki/Parkinson's_Law

"What is NaNoWriMo?" Online. Copyright 2009. September 27, 2009.
http://www.nanowrimo.org/eng/whatisnano

"Cornell College Block Plan." Online. Copyright 2009. September 27, 2009.
http://www.cornellcollege.edu/academics/ocaat/index.shtml

Skarstam, Rebecka. "Why Do We Procrastinate?" The Triple Helix. 2009. Online.
http://camtriplehelix.com/magazine/procrastinate7.pdf

Ariely D, Wertenbroch K. (2002). Procrastination, deadlines, and performance: self-control by precommitment. *Psychological Science*, 13(3):219-24.

Csikzentmihalyi, Mihaly. Flow: The Psychology of Optimal Experience. New York, NY: HarperCollins, 1990.

"Universal Law Series - Law of Expectations." Online. Copyright 2009. September 27, 2009.
http://ezinearticles.com/?Universal-Law-Series---the-Law-of-Expectation&id=78769

Christine Timko, Rudolf H. Moos, John W. Finney, Michelle D. Lesa. (2002). Long-Term Outcomes of Alcohol Use

Disorders: Comparing Untreated Individuals with Those in Alcoholics Anonymous and Formal Treatment. *Journal of Studies on Alcohol*, 61: 529-540.

Dale, Edgar. Audio-visual methods in teaching. Dryden Press, 1954.

Rosenthal, Robert, and Lenore Jacobson. Pygmalion in the Classroom: Teacher Expectation and Pupils' Intellectual Development. Norwalk, CT: Crown House Publishing, 1992.

"Amway | MLM Facts". Online. Copyright 2009. August 27, 2009.
http://www.mlmfacts.net/2009/08/the-global-top-50-mlm-companies

"If Your Goal Is Success, Don't Consult These Gurus." Online. Copyright 2009. December 18, 2007.
http://www.fastcompany.com/magazine/06/cdu.html

Matthews, Gail. "Goal Research Summary."
http://www.dominican.edu/academics/artssciences/natbehealth/psych/faculty/fulltime/gailmatthews/researchsummary2.pdf

Deutsch M, Gerard HB. (1955). A study of normative and informational social influences upon individual judgment. *Journal of Abnormal Psychology*. 51(3):629-36.

"Pareto Principle." Online. Copyright 2009. September 27, 2009.
http://en.wikipedia.org/wiki/Pareto_principle

Caildini, RB, Cacioppo, JT, Bassett, R, & Miller, JA. (1978). Low-ball procedure for producing compliance: Commitment then cost. *Journal of Personality and Social Psychology*, 36, 463-476.

Locke, EA, Latham, GP. (2002). Building a practically useful theory of goal setting and task motivation. *American Psychologist*, 57(9):705-717.

Lock, EA. (1996). Motivation through conscious goal setting. *Applied & Preventive Psychology*, 5:117-124.

Pallack, MA, Cook, CA, & Sullivan, JJ. (1980). Commitment and energy conservation. *Applied Social Psychology Annual*, 1, 235-253.

Join My Monthly Guaranteed Goals Accountability Group

"Accountability is the difference between goal setters and goal achievers."
- **Jullien Gordon**

12 Live Webinars

Every month our group will meet via online webinar to celebrate our success, evaluate our performance, deepen our understanding of the methodology, and set new goals in motion. The webinars are approximately 60 minutes each.

Online Goal Tracking System

Each month you will input your goals into our customized online goal tracking system so that you can manage your progress, document your learnings from month-to-month, and see how far you've come over the course of the year.

Online Support Group

You will have 24-7 access to our online support group. You can use it as a forum to share your successes, be inspired by others' journeys, or to ask questions and get support on your goals.

BONUS: FREE TICKET TO MY ANNUAL NYC GOAL SETTING EVENT
With your annual membership, you will also get a free ticket to my New Year Guide & Goal Setting Seminar—an annual transformative daylong life design and goal-setting experience held during the first Saturday of the year in New York City where I will personally guide you through interactive activities and introspective tools such as The New Year Guide.

www.GuaranteedGoals.com

Made in the USA
Columbia, SC
03 November 2017